D1208687

SUZANNE MILLER Exclusively distributed in Canada by MILA.

Copyright © 1989 International Copyright Ltd.

Dépôt légal, 1er trimestre 1991
Bibliothèque Nationale du Québec
ISBN 2-921354-16-0

All rights reserved throughout the world, including the USSR.

Any extract or full or partial reproduction of this work by any means whatsoever is strictly forbidden without the written permission of International Copyright Ltd.

Any unauthorized extract or reproduction by any method whatsoever constitutes copyright infringement, pursuant to the applicable sections of federal, state and provincial criminal and civil codes.

The Green Factor

Suzanne Miller

This book describes a practical method. The purpose of the method is to show you how you can earn enough money in your own home to retire as a millionaire within 5 to 10 years — and to do so effortlessly. Its author is not an accountant, attorney or legal advisor. Consequently the author (Suzanne Miller), the distributor in Canada (MILA) and the publisher (International Copyright Ltd.) discharge themselves of any liability or obligation associated with any loss or risk which might directly or indirectly result from the information presented in this book.

If you require legal, accounting, or any other kind of advice, please contact a professional in the appropriate field.

In my capacity as Ms. Suzanne Miller's accountant, I certify that the former has earned more than 1 million dollars in 34 months through her method. I certify that Ms. Miller's testimonial is authentic. I also certify that all of the other projections of earnings are fully achievable.

D. Hamlet, Accountant

Preface

HOW TO DO IT ALL FOR FREE

What can be done for money can also often be done for free, and sometimes much more effectively. In the following pages, I'm going to describe a step-by-step process which can make you rich.

In Chapter XI (I like saving the best news for last), I tell you how to do all of this *without spending a penny*.

So read on. The fact the you may not have any money now should not discourage you. Remember, I started out without a cent. How to do so is as surprisingly simple as method itself, and I'll spell it out for you in Chapter XI.

Introduction

Dear Reader,

My name is Suzanne Miller. Before I discovered my method, I think I was like a lot of folks. I hadn't gotten much schooling. I'd been working in a shoe factory for 6 years. Before that, I'd been a housekeeper for 2 years and waitressed for another 2 1/2. Plus, I'd been unemployed twice, for 6-month periods. I'd spent over 10 years working like a fool earning practically nothing, for awful bosses. I got divorced real young and had to take care of my children myself. We never had enough money to get through the month. The bills piled up each day. My telephone line was cut more often than it was connected. I spent most of my spare time trying to borrow money from my folks, friends and neighbors. This whole situation lasted more than 11 years. Then one day I decided I was fed up, quit — and decided to take my life into my own hands.

A few days before I quit, I borrowed $20,000 from my friends and the bank to start up an import company. I managed to lose $12,000 in the company's first 2 months of operations. It went bankrupt.

Then I somehow managed to scrape together another $45,000 to start a mail order business for classy European clothing. That was a complete disaster. I lost $37,000 over the next 4 months. With the money that I had to borrow from my family just to live, I was then $56,000 in the red.

Obviously, I was so much in the hole at this point that no one was going to lend me any more money. And the law was trying to seize what little property I had left.

I did nothing, at that point, except spend entire days trying to think of ways to pull myself out of the mess I was in. And on day four, in the middle of the afternoon, I got an incredible idea. I'll never forget that moment. I said to myself, back then, that perhaps I'd just discovered the simplest way in the world to get rich quickly. It was so simple, that at first sight, it seemed too good to be true. But I was able to start putting it into action — from my very own home — the next morning. And, I calculated that I would probably be able to earn several hundred dollars per day within the following 48 hours — and several thousands of dollars per week, by the end of the first week. I was still figuring out all the details, which were a bit hazy to me, I admit, so I spent the evening working it my plan out on paper. And after I did, I looked at the results and was sure. There was no question that it would succeed! Although I must confess, I could hardly believe it. The next morning, after an almost sleepless night, I put my discovery to work for me.

I brought in $410 within the first 48 hours. I earned almost $4,000 the first week. And I put away $26,521 at the end of the first month. It had previously taken me two years to earn that much.

I was able to repay almost half my debts the first month.

Then I went out and bought the newest Jaguar off the dealer's lot: a little life-long dream I'd had. Within six months I'd earned more than I could have made any other way the rest of my life. I paid off the rest of my $56,000 debt and bought a beautiful $300,000 home. The bank manager, of course, was a bit more than astonished, every time I came in to make a deposit.

I made a fortune publishing and selling "How To" books. This report will show you how to do the same yourself. To begin with, I'd like to point out a few of the benefits of this profession:

*It requires little time to succeed. A few hours per week are enough. You do it when it's best for you, whatever days you like. I rarely put in more than 4 hours a day or a total of more than 20 a week. I took long holidays: 8 weeks in the summer, 4 at Christmas and 4 at Easter. You can do use my method and keep on with your current job, if you want. You could do it after work or on the weekend.

*You don't need any start-up money. You don't even have to take out a loan. I was $56,000 in debt when I started, and didn't ask anyone for an additional cent, but I was able to make $410 the first 2 days, $3,916 the first week and a grand total of $26,521 the first month.

*You don't need any experience or special knowledge to let it to work for you. Frankly, I don't even have a high school diploma, and I have no prior experience in my field.

*You can work at home, or anywhere else. It doesn't matter where you live, and you can even use the method while you're away on vacation, down on the beach or out camping! I brought in more than $11,000 one astounding week — while I was off on a trip to Mexico.

*What's more, it's all entirely honest and absolutely legal.

*Since it's so simple, you can be any age and do it. Retired folks and teenagers can make the same kind of money I have. No physical effort is required. Men and women are equally able to apply it. For instance one woman made $120,000 last year, and she's 68!

*This is a completely new, unique and previously unknown system. And I can assure you, there are no real estate, pyramid, door-to-door or telephone sales involved. This is something completely different. It's much simpler than any of that and can bring in far more money. With no risk whatsoever.

*You don't need an office or any equipment. You don't have to buy or rent a thing. I started doing this three years ago in my own home and I still work out of my own home.

As you can see, this report will show you how to start up a business publishing and selling "How To" books.

At first glance, the report takes the form of a book — the kind you might find in any bookstore. But the comparison stops there. This book is very specific and much more practical than anything you could buy in a bookstore. In it, I've specified everything that I did, step by step, in easy-to-understand, practical and clear language, so anyone could understand and apply my method immediately — with instant results. The information it provides will enable you to get started in this field. Everything you need to know is included in this book. With it, you should be able to begin earning huge amounts of money within a few weeks — without taking any risks and working at home, when you like. Many have earned fortunes this way.

I personally earned $318,000 the first year and $451,000 the second. And I was working less than 20 hours per week, with 16 weeks of vacation each year.

Since this New Year's Day, I've earned more than

$400,000. That averages out to $50,000 per month — this year. I'm confident I'll make another $500,000 by the end of the year.

But I want to be clear about one thing. I will not promise absolutely anyone that he or she will earn as much as I have with this system. On the other hand, I am convinced — and I can honestly guarantee — that this system will make from $50,000 to $250,000 per year for anyone who employs it. $50,000 is the absolute bottomline for anyone working at home. And I'll say it once again, to be clear: ANYONE CAN EARN A MINIMUM $50,000 PER YEAR WITH THIS SYSTEM — EFFORTLESSLY.

That is a minimum. I would say $100,000 to $150,000 per year is the average. You may also earn far more than this.

For example: over the past 3 years, I've only let a dozen or so of my friends in on my method. One of them earned more than a half-million dollars, and another earned $230,000 in their first year. The least successful made $72,000 in year one and nearly $250,000 over the past 2 1/2 years.

I would go so far as saying that, if you only put my advice to work for you 10 hours a week, 8 months a year, it will be virtually impossible for you to earn less than $50,000 a year.

The only thing you need is this book — and to apply the practical advice contained in it. *Read it in full* and take notes. *You should reread the book several times* so that you fully integrate the advice it contains.

However: don't quit your job until this method is enabling you to earn AT LEAST 4 times more than your present salary. This is an important precaution.

I hope that the publication and sale of "How To" books will be just as successful for you as it has been for other fortunate people today.

From this point on, everything depends on you. Read this book and take your first big step towards fortune.

Good luck!

Suzanne Miller.

Chapter 1

GETTING THE INFORMATION

Before you go out and start accumulating information, you should select a topic for your book. This topic must be one of substantial interest to many people. Studies have shown that huge numbers of people will pay large sums to obtain certain kinds of information. "How To" books provide such information — and are thus of interest to a significant portion of the population.

Before deciding the subject to work on, make sure that it meets the following criteria:

It must be of substantial interest to many people.

It must not be a topic on which widespread information is already available. Exclusivity will do much to enhance its value.

It must be easy to research and write about.

It must not be costly to produce or to send by mail.

You must be able to sell it for at least 3 times any costs you may have producing it.

Many topics meet these requirements. Studies and experience have shown that the most popular books fall under the following headings:

How to test your own I.Q.
How to give yourself a personality test
How to stop smoking
How to become famous
How to become a detective
How to work in radio
How to work in television
How to sell used books
How to provide storage space
How to start an ad agency
How to win contests
How to become an accountant
How to get a promotion
How to find a job
How to train horses
How to repair clothing
How to earn your living drawing caricatures
How to open a souvenir shop
How to age gracefully
How to make friends
How to increase your sales volume
How to start a small magazine
How to move to Europe
How to learn kung fu
How to learn jujitsu
How to learn judo
How to hypnotize people
How to become an artist
How to play the piano
How to play the guitar

How to start an import business
How to start an export business
How to improve your personality
How to sell correspondence courses
How to become an investment counselor
How to start a counseling center
How to open a dating agency
How to repair works of art
How to write personal notes
How to start a cooking school
How to start a sewing school
How to start an art school
How to run an art gallery
How to become an antique dealer
How to become a wine taster
How to evaluate franchise offers
How to raise dogs
How to raise rabbits
How to move to Australia
How to become a real estate broker
How to become a travel agent
How to become a reporter
How to cut your taxes
How to express yourself
How to interpret dreams
How to reduce stress
How to raise a child

If you want to succeed in this field, you should select one of these topics. As studies have clearly demonstrated their popularity, you'll be most likely to succeed if one of them serves as the foundation for your first book. You should have little trouble researching and writing about these subjects, as long as you employ a bit of creativity.

Once you've selected your topic, you'll need to research it, so you can later write about it. There are many ways to carry out your research.

You'll start at the public library with its vast store of information. Ask the librarian where to get the facts on your subject. Read or skim through all the books associated with it. Take notes on anything that appears useful.

Then, order any books, reports or material that may supplement this information. You must fully document your subject. If necessary, find a consultant in the field to provide you with further assistance.

You can also take courses, go to conferences and attend seminars on your subject. One thing is very important: keep up to date on anything new in this field.

I realize this will involve a certain amount of reading and study. But you can earn between $50,000 and $250,000 for a single book. Doesn't that make it worth the trouble? Your investment will be minuscule compared with your profits. Later, I'll even show you how to do all of this without spending a single penny.

As you can see, it's all quite simple.

Once you've done your research and taken notes, you should be on top of your subject. Keep your notes in a safe place. Later I'll show you how to compile them into a book, step by step. You'll be able to write this book without knowing the first thing about being a writer. Most of your work involves research. Once that's accomplished, putting the information you've collected into a book will be one of the easiest tasks you've ever accomplished.

Chapter 2

WRITING YOUR ADS OR HAVING THEM WRITTEN

Your books sales will depend on how well you advertise. The ad is the single most important element in this project. It is what will or will not enable you to succeed. It is crucial that your advertising be geared to one thing and one thing only — selling your book. Consequently, you should either learn how to write your ads yourself, or you should get a professional to do it for you.

In my opinion, if you can afford to pay a good copywriter to produce your ads, this is the wisest course of action. These people know how to play with words to obtain the best results: that's their job. If you break an arm, you go visit the doctor. If you have a toothache, you go to a dentist. So if you need some good advertising work, it makes sense to have a copywriter do it for you. You may spend a little more money, but the results should more than compensate for it. The better the ad, the more your business. If you don't happen to know a professional copywriter, any other good writer could do. But make sure you see some samples and are sure of his or her rates. Look around and decide on the best price-quality ratio.

But, if you know you can do a good job, *then you can produce your own ad copy, yourself — FOR FREE.* Professionals are important, but they are not the be-all and end-all. You can do also do an excellent job. But to do so, you have to know what makes people look at, read and believe ads.

In the next chapter, I'm going to give you a brief tutorial on advertising. It will tell you everything you need to know for generating good ads.

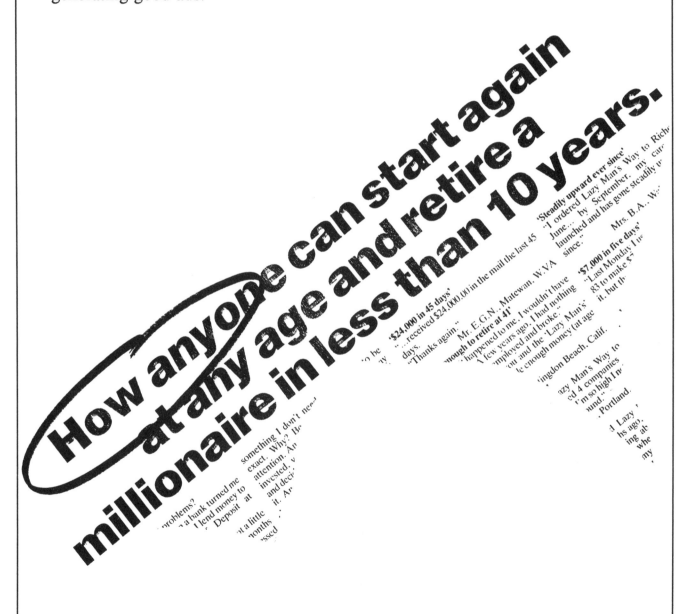

CHAPTER 3

HOW TO WRITE AND PRESENT AN AD OR A MAIL-ORDER LETTER

If your ad grabs the reader, the likelihood of you selling your book will increase greatly. Remember: the ad is your key to success.

WRITING YOUR AD

Your working tools are:
(a) a set of published ads
(b) different writing techniques
(c) your intuition

(a) COLLECTING ADS

You should make it a habit to read ads. Start off browsing through newspapers in your bookstore or library and making notes of the best ads.

Look at all of the ads first, to get a sense of their diversity.

Check the entire paper. Don't be limited by your personal tastes. Try to get a general knowledge of the kinds of products and services offered through advertising.

Clip out or copy any ad that catches your eye. Start building a well-organized ad collection. It will be useful as a reference tool. It's good to know what others have done before you. Once you have a general feel for writing styles, you can start breaking down your collection into subject and quality headings. Use the best ads you've found as a model for your own. Take the poor ones and rewrite them, to see how you could have gotten the message across better. As your skills improve, so will your editing techniques.

(b) DIFFERENT WRITING STYLES

The different writing styles I am about to recommend have been based on extensive copywriter research and experience. Advertising copy is, quite naturally, a key factor in a product's success. Knowing how to write a good ad obviously requires a certain basic technical knowledge. I'll list the most important techniques and you should become thoroughly familiar with them. Once you've practiced them a bit, you'll soon realize how easy it is to dash out a powerful ad.

Even before an ad is read, it must be seen and believed. Readers must become interested on seeing the first line. If an ad is going to work, it requires a catchy headline. Headlines stimulate readers' imaginations and promise them that their wishes will come true.

These promises must be based on reader needs. People read advertisements because of what they want. Therefore, they must be promised things that they want. You must speak TO THE READER and NOT TO YOURSELF. You can do this most easily by putting yourself in the reader's shoes: what does he or she want?

In order to get the reader's attention, promise savings, earnings or achievements. A product's benefits must stand out. Enhance the product through the judicious description of its special features. It's not up to the reader to guess what the product might do: you must say it. You must clearly show the reader what the product can do.

(1) THE TEASER (THE HEADLINE)

As a general rule, headlines should be a maximum of 8 words. They should guarantee readers: (1) certain benefits, (2) the avoidance of inconvenience, (3) or describe some novel product or service.

The teaser should be written in the imperative. Telling readers to do something gives much more weight to your ad.

Think up a few good teasers. But bear in mind that they must:
* qualify your reader
* make a promise
* made the reader curious
* make the promise believable

Here are a few techniques that will let you grab a reader's attention with the headline.

THE INTERROGATIVE APPROACH

Questions are one of the most popular headline techniques. It should be structured so that a reader's answer will always be positive. Here are a few sample expressions found in ad headlines:

* Did you know that...?
* How...?
* Why...?

* How much...?
* What do you have...?

THE NOVELTY APPROACH

The headline will offer some kind of novel service or product that should interest the reader.

THE SUMMARY APPROACH

The offer's key features should be summarized so that they will tickle the reader's fancy.

THE TESTIMONIAL APPROACH

A testimonial from a satisfied customer can be used as a teaser. The reader will identify with that person and thus be more convinced by the offer.

Don't think about your ad for a day or so before you write its headline. And once you've made a few tentative choices, ask your friends or family which they like best.

Eliminate all but the best of these possible headlines. But don't throw the others away: you may want to use them if you ever rerum the ad.

A major portion of the time that goes into writing an ad is devoted to finding the right headline — that's what determines if the ad is read or not. If the headline is only so-so, you'll lose 80% of your potential readership.

(2) THE OFFER

Making a good offer is a crucial element in your success. The better your offer, the more money you'll make. There are several components involved in the offer. Here are a few of them:

Your product price must be attractive — and preferably irresistible — to the reader. However, a reason for this excellent value must be given. For example, if you advertise:

SPECIAL PRICE

the bargain should be justified with a reason such as:

SPECIAL PROMOTIONAL OFFER
INVENTORY CLEARANCE
MINOR MANUFACTURING DEFECTS

and so on.

Monthly payments may be offered where larger sums are involved. This kind of payment scheme requires good accounting. I recommend that you ask for about 30% of the price as the initial payment.

- Large companies even offer limited free trial offers. If the customer is satisfied, he or she keeps the product and pays, or otherwise, returns the merchandise.

- Guarantees are sometimes essential. They reassure clients, since the seller has shown good faith. Guarantees vary depending on the product offered. They can range from a promise to repair certain portions of the product, a refund in full ("satisfaction guaranteed or your money back"), or an exchange.

- Offers can be valid for a limited time only. Providing a time limit forces the reader to make a quick decision. He or she will think the offer is so good, it won't last for long. It might be even more profitable to specify the exact date at which an offer expires. Special limited duration offers are a classic product promotion technique. This method has been well borne out by experience and is still as effective today as ever.

- Offering a present with any purchase can also substantially boost sales. Such offers are of particular benefit with new clients, and helps break down their sales resistance.

All of these different kinds of techniques may be combined. When you are putting together an offer, keep your eyes open for other well worded offers. But be careful. You must make sure that your offer makes sense — otherwise your reader may not believe it. A good offer is half the sale, thus the key to success.

(3) READABILITY

If you want your ad to be seen, it's got to be readable. This means it should be easy to read, understand and remember. In order to achieve this goal, you have to keep rereading, rewriting and improving your text, and getting your friends' opinions as you go along.

With small ads, you're limited by space, so you'll have to be brief and clear. In other words: cut any fat out of your message.

But don't, as a result, give it the telegraphic style that is typical of classified ads.

Avoid abbreviations. They introduce confusion. Maybe you'll pay a bit more to write your text in full (ad rates are based on numbers of lines), but at least the ad will be readable and understandable. And your potential number of buyers will increase.

Short, simple sentences produce clearer ads. Try not to use more than 15 words per sentence. And be careful about punctuation: bad use will obscure your message.

(C) INTUITION

Listen to your own hunches. Once you've assembled a collection of ads and writing styles, it will serve as a guide for creating your own material. There is no "foolproof" way to write the perfect ad. But, the more your knowledge and experience, the better you're likely to do. Particularly if you keep your critical faculties turned on.

HOW TO PROPERLY LAYOUT AN AD

Once you've carefully composed your text, you must organize it well visually. This is what lures readers from the start. A reader either does or does not look at an ad based on its location, its form and its contents. The ad's layout should make people want to read it. The wording should correspond with the ad's overall visual impression, its color and its other aesthetic elements. Together, they can combine to produce a highly appealing message.

Consequently, an ad's layout is crucial to good visual impact. Here are a few techniques that will make it possible to boost an ad's performance, and thereby multiply your potential number of customers.

(A) WHERE TO PLACE AN AD IN A PUBLICATION

Where you place an advertisement in a newspaper or magazine is fairly important, since it can have a great influence on your of success.

First of all, you must decide whether you'll advertise in daily papers or magazines. This decision should be based on the kind of offer you're making. If you want the ad to appear repeatedly, you can use magazines or papers (or both). If you prefer a particular day or several non-consecutive ones, you'll need to print the ad in daily papers.

If you've decided to publish it in a daily, you've next got to determine the day on which it should appear. Wednesday and Saturdays are generally considered to be best.

There are very few publications that don't carry ads. It's crucial to make the right choice of publication, and a wide range is available. The one you want will have a readership that corresponds as closely as possible with the your target audience. Speaking to the right customer base will significantly enhance your results.

Whether you decide on daily newspapers or magazines, you should also consider the best times of year to run ads.

Once you've selected the publication had been selected, you must carefully decide where exactly to situate the ad, to maximize its impact. An advertiser is entitled to place an ad on almost any page.

If the advertised product is aimed at a limited clientèle, the ad should be placed in the section that best corresponds with the interests of your target audience.

If the product or service will be of interest to most of the publication's readers, you should advertise on one of its first few pages. These are the ones with the greatest exposure.

As a general rule, whatever section you select, the higher an ad is located on a page, the better its chances of success.

It is also better to advertise on right-hand pages, then left-hand ones. Studies show that readers pay more attention to these pages. Consequently, there's a much better chance your ad will be seen on a right-hand page.

If the ad contains a clip-out mail-in coupon, put it near the outside of the page.

You should consider the cost of advertising space. Space rates depend on the type of publication, its circulation, its size, and the page selected. Newspapers and magazines will be pleased to send you rate sheets.

If an advertiser can't afford, or doesn't want to risk a large ad for financial reasons, classified ads are a much less costly alternative. Classified enable advertisers to gradually build up profits to subsequently pay for bigger ads. *This is a prudent way of starting up FOR FREE.*

And if an advertiser is not confident enough of his or her message to pay for a large space, the classifieds can be used to test different versions of the ad. The best performer can then be rerun as a big ad.

In short: where you put your ad is a significant factor its yield. But that's not all. Once an advertiser has carefully selected an ad's location, he or she has to know how to use that space to its utmost.

(B) VISUAL ASPECTS OF THE TEXT

Once an advertiser has the right text and the right space, he or she should lay it out well. In other words, it's crucial that the text be read, be understood — and be convincing. Layout helps achieve these objectives by grabbing the reader's attention and making the message stand out loud and clear. These dual objectives must be respected, since there's no point in publishing a good ad that a reader will neither see nor understand. Properly arranging a text's visual appearance will increase its advertising impact. A text must be just as clear in its appearance as it is in its meaning.

An ad's location is important in terms of: (1) layout, and (2) lettering.

(1) LAYOUT

As we have already noted, the ad's headline is the key

element in attracting a reader's attention. Consequently, the space is occupies must be proportional to its relative importance in the ad. It is generally centered and located at the top of the ad. It could, however, be set along the right or left margins.

Sufficient blank space should be left around the headline so that it clearly stands out.

The text in the body of the ad is much smaller than that of the headline — but must still be legible. If you want your prospective customer to read all the way through your ad, leave ample space between paragraphs. This will highlight each element of your offer. It's not the reader's job to decipher your text and figure out which elements of the offer are attractive. The text's layout is supposed to make this information easily accessible.

(2) LETTERING

You can substantially alter your ad's appearance through different kinds of lettering. Here is a bit of advice on the use of character style that will substantially boost impact.

The headline should always be in the biggest and thickest letters. This will make it easy to see.

Different fonts (character styles) will also make certain portions of the text stand out.

In general, however, a light and breezy font is recommended. This will make it easier to highlight key elements of the offer, with capitals or bolds. Certain advertisers prefer italics. We don't, since we find them hard to read.

The text should start off with an ornamental capital (an initial letter of text that is 4 to 5 times larger than its companions).

By following the above guidelines, you can produce an attractive ad, merely by using the appropriate type styles and organizing them effectively. Keep in mind the importance of proper spacing and the use of different fonts to emphasize key elements.

(3) GRAPHIC ASPECTS OF AN AD

A few graphic highlights can significantly contribute to your ad's performance. However, they must be used judiciously. Their purpose it to make the text more attractive — not to make it gaudy. If misused, they will overshadow your message. The key issue is to make sure the meaning is clear and the general appearance of the ad is well balanced.

Bearing in mind that graphics must be used appropriately, here are a few examples of what they are, and why and how to use them:

UNDERLINING

Underlining is a basic way of highlighting certain words and phrases. Before using it, you should decide what needs underlining. Then reduce this potential to the essential words you want to stand out.

PICTURES

Pictures display what the ad has to offer. If well chosen, they will enhance an ad. They can take the form of photos or drawings. Obviously, they should be clear and sharp. If your ad will be in black and white, your original pictures should be black and white. This will help maintain good contrast. Color photos printed in black and white often turn out muddy.

FRAMES

Frames can highlight an entire ad or certain portions of it, such as the headline, the guarantee, the price, a picture, etc.

You can do frames by hand. Consequently, they are a fairly simple means of providing graphic enhancements to an ad and generating a professional look. Even better, and less time consuming results may be obtained with the wide range of commercial paste-on frames that are available at a stationery or graphic supply store.

COLORS

Color advertising often looks better than that in black and white. Two factors must be considered before opting for color. One is the much higher cost involved. The other is how well the product offered will look in color.

In other words, you should calculate how much better your sales will be if you use color instead of black and white.

Color may be an essential factor in the promotion of certain products. However, we feel that a thorough assessment of increased potential should be made before deciding to advertise in color.

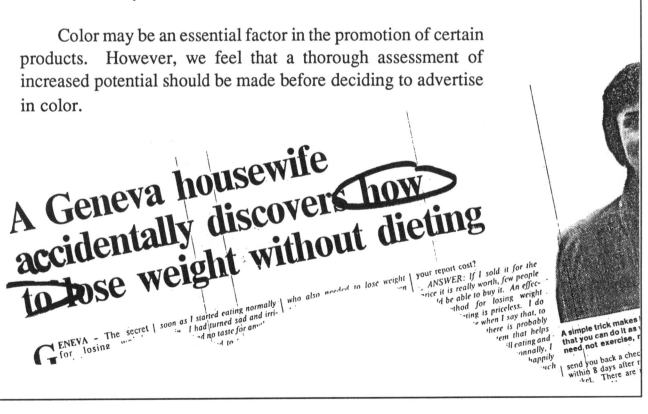

Chapter 4

MAIL ORDER SALES

We explained in the previous chapter how you can promote your book through newspaper ads. This chapter describes another sales technique: mail order. The letter you send should be written based on the advertising principles discussed in Chapter 3.

The advantage of this process is that it is a much more personal way of selling than newspaper ads. With it, you can communicate directly with your potential customers, at their homes.

Your mailing kit should consist of the following:
* #10 window envelopes
* #6 reply envelopes
* order coupons
* promotional letters

You have to start off by contacting a printer, who will ultimately produce your direct mailing materials. Explain your plans and ask any questions you might have. Your printer will be pleased to advise you and help you produce an excellent mailing. You might wish to talk with several, to get the best price-quality ratio.

Many of those who receive your letter will barely give it 5 seconds of thought before tossing it into the wastebasket. But you can increase your percentages by including a short teaser in the window envelope (see the previous chapter). This will encourage people to open it. Once they do so, your letterhead should impress them enough so they'll want to read it. I've provided an example of a how the outside of an envelope should look on the next page.

(a) Print a slanted teaser on the window envelope.

(b) Include a small picture of a man and woman hauling their money off to the bank on the bottom right of this envelope.

A few minor additions like this will increase your rate of response and further increase your profits.

Chapter 5

AD LAYOUT

Once you've written your ad, you'll typeset it. Certain copywriters, as well as print shops, are equipped to provide this service.

Just bring the ad's text to your printer, along with some sample ads whose typesetting you like. You'll find such samples in newspapers, magazines and direct mailings sent to you. Talk to your printer and describe the general appearance you want for your ad. Then specify print size and headlines style, spacing and characters fonts (appearance).

I would recommend that you use the following lettering sizes for your ads:

* 24 points for the headline
* 12 to 18 points for section headings
* 10 points for the text

The term "point" is used in printing with respect to type

sizes. Your printer will understand it.

The same printer you may have used for your envelopes can take care of this job, as well. Make sure, though, that he is able to do what you ask. And feel free to compare prices. Check with different newspapers, as they may also be able to typeset and layout your ads.

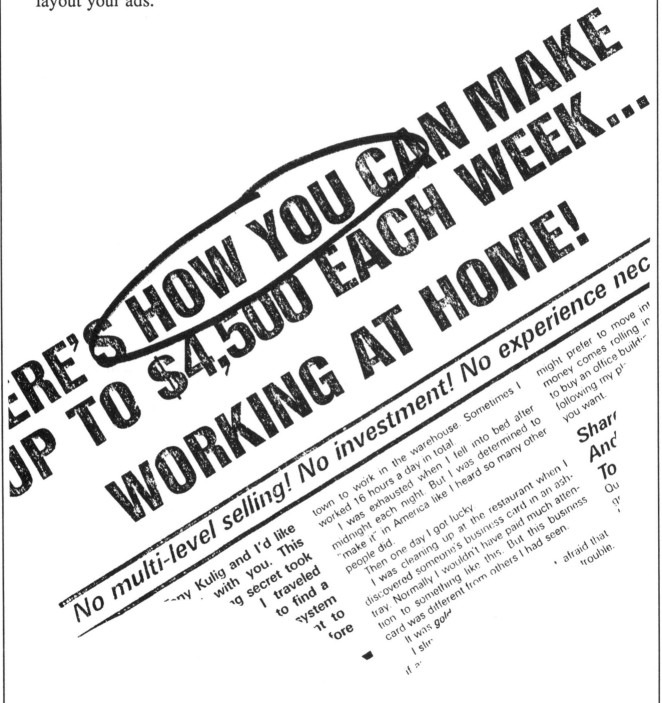

Chapter 6

WRITING THE BOOK

If you can talk into a microphone, you can write a book. Anyone can write a book. But before getting started, you should pull out all the information you've collected and go over it again. In order to dictate a book, you have to be very familiar with your subject.

To begin with, you'll need about 10 sheets of paper or index cards. Since you're thoroughly familiar with your subject, break down the information relating to it into about 10 categories. Then, give each category a title which briefly and clearly captures its essence. Write these titles at the top of each blank piece of paper.

All of your sheets now have titles. Write 5 to 20 subtitles on each sheet that further define each category. This will clear up in your mind what belongs in each section of your book, and prompt your memory for everything that you've read on the subject.

Now you'll have 8 to 10 sheets with 5 to 10 subheadings each. Spread the sheets out in front of you. Take the first sheet and get your recorder ready. Read the title and subheadings aloud. This will help you remember what you've read on a particular subject. Now take the microphone and talk about what you know on your topic. If you've carefully studied your information, you should recall it easily, without looking at your notes. Do this for each of the 8 to 10 sections. Use simple, clear language. Speak as if you were talking to a friend. In other words: be relaxed. Do this all the way through to the end.

Your titles will become chapter headings. Consequently, your book will have 8 to 10 chapters. But this number is not an absolute. Use the actual number you need (whether it's more or less than this) to explain your subject well.

You've now composed your first book. And all that you needed to do was to speak into a microphone.

Chapter 7

FROM THE RECORDING TO THE COMPLETED MANUSCRIPT

You've recorded your book on cassette. Now it's time to transcribe it on a typewriter. Some writers can do this job for you: transform your recording into a ready-to-print manuscript.

The text can be typed in either an 8   1/2" x 11" or a 6" x 9" format. These are the most common.

Once the manuscript is complete, correct any errors and make any necessary changes. Reread the text carefully. And, if possible, have someone else as well go over it for you. You might ask a university student to correct the punctuation, spelling, grammar, etc.

How to Become a "Non-Degree" Engineer in the Booming World of Electronics

Thousands of real engineering jobs are being filled by men without engineering degrees. The pay is good, the future bright. Here's how to qualify...

By G. O. ALLEN
President, Cleveland Institute of Electronics

THE BIG BOOM IN ELECTRONICS—and the shortage of graduate engineers—new breed of professional engineer. He has achieve with

How to make up to $250 a day in your own business right away in good times or bad

For Fast Service call toll free hours, or operate better

make that much—or carpet, upholstery stores. You an you

MEN – WOMEN

LEARN HOW TO GET RICH

Get rich! How? One sure way is to have your rich uncle mention you in his Will. Not too practical! How about a proved way to riches that's wide open to you today! World Trade/Mail Order to get rich I

using my over 30 years of experience and my proved methods that have brought such cess to so many ambitious men and women! The Mellinger Plan is like having an experienced friend guiding your every step to keep you on the profit track!

Products to deal in! I start you $1,000 hottest new Imports

Chapter 8

THE BIRTH OF YOUR BOOK

Once your manuscript has been fully revised and corrected, it's ready to print as a book. This is a job for a printer. As before, check with several (you can find them in the Yellow Pages) and select the one with the best price-quality ratio.

Once your book is typeset, your printer will send you the proofs to check. You can then prepare any illustrations, placing appropriate pictures in blank spaces on the proofs. Pay special attention to your cover. The right look will make it appear all that much more professional.

Bring all of this material back to the printer and order the smallest possible run. Once your orders have built up, you can print more later on.

At the same time you print your book, get envelopes in which to mail it. Print "BOOK RATE" on them. This will entitle you to much lower postal fees.

"How To Get Rich Sooner Than You

A year ago, I was barely making enough to s

"How I Earned A Hal Million Dollars In T Last Six Months . . . effortlessly and by workin ly 5 to 10 hou

"HOW TO MAKE $2,000 A WEEK SELLING INFORMATION BY MAIL
by RUSS VON HOELSCHER

(A Reg. $12 Value — Now Yours for the Asking —

USINESS OR SHEER MADNESS?

his: Best-selling author and mail order marketing
uss von Hoelscher spends several months writing
ering materials for a new book, *HOW TO MAKE
WEEK SELLING INFORMATION BY MAIL.*
120-page book is typeset and printed at a total

For over 20 years, Russ von Ho
scher has helped thousands
ambitious men and women g
started in a profitable business

Chapter 9

ADVERTISE YOUR BOOK BY MAIL

THROUGH DIRECT MAILINGS

Once you've printed your letters and envelopes (see Chapter 4), all you have to do is mail them. If your printer is far from your home, just call and ask that your letters and envelopes be forwarded to your mailing service.

The mailing service will stuff your window envelopes with your letters, reply coupons, and reply envelopes, and then send them off for you. They do this mechanically, with specially designed equipment. They will store your packages while waiting for your mailing list.

Now you're ready to order a mailing list of potential customers. Many mail-order companies rent such lists, so you won't have much trouble finding one. Send the list to your mailing service as quickly as possible. When you rent the lists, you should specify that you want names on adhesive labels. Your mailer will stick them on your mailing and send them off to your prospects.

All you have to do now is wait for the replies and cheques to start coming in. Try to fill yours orders as quickly as possible. Send off the merchandise quickly, so you won't receive complaints.

Here is a bit of additional information:

You should sell your book for from $10 to $25. Research has shown that this is the best price range for mail-ordered "How To" books. Your price may be relatively high, as you are contacting a specific group of people and offering them an exclusive product.

Obtain lists of names of people who have already ordered products worth from $15 to $25. This will guarantee that your ad will be addressed to a specific target group, which should help boost sales. You'll have a higher rate of response. Bear in mind that if someone has already made a mail-order purchase, he or she is very likely to make another.

Try to make sure that your ad really corresponds with your book. Give your customers the best book you can. That way, you'll keep your customers satisfied and avoid having too many returns. Give people their moneys' worth. The price of your book is determined by its number of pages, but by the quality of information it contains.

THROUGH ADVERTISING

If you advertise your book in newspapers, you should sell it for from $10 to $20. If you decide to print newspaper ads, your strategy may vary a bit from that described above. You'll be communicating with a mass market audience — with people who are not particularly interested in mail order purchases. Your advertising has got to be very attractive to them. It should be laid out in several columns (as are newspaper articles). In the lower right-hand corner, include a clip-out coupon with the address for ordering your book. Use a standard typeface similar to that of the paper in which you are advertising. This will make your advertising fit in better with the newspaper's look. In short, use the same approach you see in other mail-order ads.

Once your ad is ready, call the advertising section of the newspaper in which you are interested, and ask for their advertising rates.

It might be useful, at this point, to register an advertising company in your name. Registering a company at your town hall or registry bureau only costs a few dollars and takes a few minutes. Advertising your newly created advertising company will often save you 15% on your ad rates. Just give a copy of the registration form to the newspapers with which you are doing business. But bear in mind that not every single paper will give you this 15% cut.

You should let as many people as possible know about your book. Saturate the market. And when you make money, don't go out and spend it all on personal things. Reinvest it in lists of names and advertisements. This will let you earn your money quickly. You'll make huge amounts: $60,000 in 2 months is a very realistic figure. The only requirement is for your book to sell well. Many become millionaires with this method. It's a profession that will let you get rich — quickly.

One last piece of advice: don't advertise in December or July. These are the worst months for selling "How To" books.

Chapter 10

FILLING YOUR ORDERS

By now, most of your work has been done. The last stage is *CASHING YOUR CHECKS*. If your ad was good, you should have received lots of reply coupons and cheques. You can answer them yourself, or hire someone to help you do so. Or, you can hire a mailing firm to respond to all of your orders. Just provide them with the envelopes and books.

Make sure you hold onto your customers' names. You'll be able to use them for subsequent books, and also *rent them to mailing list companies FOR BIG BUCKS*.

How to get rich

...wanted to go into business for yourself?
...ll set you up and back you in
...ur own. Mail the... mail or-

ADVERTISEMENT

ADVERT

How to make others secretly DO YOUR BID
with the astonishing power of
AUTOMATIC MIND COMMA

Here's how to get started in just 3 minutes...

...riend:

...ne. I... is about to leap into your life...
...way to control the thoughts and
...ther... without their knowing it...
...om all w... h they may *not* want to fol-
...they carry them out to a

...U CAN SHARE ...and" you'll be
...ogram gets you starte... turn on The
... - even while holding ...drop every-
...h hundreds of orders. We d... idea
...to invest a cent in merchat... of
...4 magazines gives you $200 ...

your neighbors won't say... your boss keeps
quiet about... ALL BROUGHT INTO THE
OPEN JUST FOR YOU!! They'll tell you all
their secrets, but they won't know why.
Hold on now, because I haven't told you yet
about the best part of "Automatic Mind-C...
mand."
You may have to bolt your d...
...ple from overwhelming ...
...ors, rewards! Perf...
up to you an...
anythin...

EXCITING SECRETS REVEAL WAY...

How to get rich now

...a small, cool pond, I sat down on a big
rock and stared into the clear water.
Amazing idea hits
...udden, the idea hit me, like a
...I seen it before? My
...as breathless.

How To Find A Husba

In One Year ...or less GUARANTEED!!!

Husband
or Your Mone...

Chapter 11

HOW TO START-UP WITHOUT A PENNY

Once you've decided to launch your mail-order "How To" book company, you might wonder where you'll get the money to start up. Here are ways:

* Invest in classified ads
* Get a bank loan
* Borrow money from friends
* Find investors
* Make an offer to an existing firm

Each of these alternatives lets you get started *without a penny of your own money.*

In the first case, you'll ask your printer for "60 days net" credit terms. This will let you earn enough money with this method to pay off its costs — before they're due. Order a small print run at first. Once demand for your book has been demonstrated, you can reprint it in larger quantities.

(1) INVEST IN CLASSIFIED ADS

This method is neither new nor costly. It is, however, highly effective. You can usually pay for classified ads 30 days after they appear. This gives you a sensible way to test your book's sales.

If you pay for your ads in 30 days and your printer in 60, *you will not have spent a single cent.*

(2 & 3) TAKE OUT A BANK LOAN, OR BORROW FROM FRIENDS

You'll be able to finance your overhead costs (stamps, envelopes, etc.) *without spending a penny* if your bank manger or friends agree to a small loan. Once again, *you will not have laid out any money.*

(4) FIND INVESTORS

Once you have completed your book and written the ad and/ or mail-order letter for it, you should prepare a *project summary*. It should be clear, precise and well presented.

Then show it to one or more investors.

Who are these investors? They can be anyone. They are people who have money and are looking for folks like yourself so that they can invest and make more money than they would in the bank.

If your project summary seems interesting, they'll be ready to invest in you. If the tests run well and profits are earned quickly, they'll be ready to invest even more, so that the business will increase even more rapidly in size. Let's take an example:

You find 3 investors ready to put $2,000 a piece in your project. You sign a contract with them guaranteeing that they can have their $2,000 bank in X months and that they'll each be entitled to 25% of the profits. 3 x 25% = 75%, which leaves 25% for you!

That 25% is what you earn for your idea and work.

This is just a general example showing how you can earn lots of money without laying out a single penny.

(5) MAKE AN OFFER TO AN EXISTING MAIL-ORDER HOUSE

There are hundreds of mail-order companies in America on the lookout for new products. Call a few and suggest your book. If they turn you down, it's probably either because your book isn't good enough or the advertising has to be improved. If that's the case, they're probably right. After all, they're the experts.

Once you find a company that's interested in your book, sign a contract with them.

Ask for between 1% and 5% of the gross, or 5% to 25% of the net profits from the sale of your book. This will provide you with income for months or years — with no additional work on your part required. All you will have to have done will be to create a book and write the advertising for it. The mail-order company will market and finance it. All you'll have to do from then on is take your money to the bank.

Hundreds of products are sold by the millions — *through mail order*. Imagine what a $20 book can do for you, even if you're only getting 3% of the gross. 3% of $20 million = *$600,000*! That should be enough for you to retire. It's certainly worth working just a few days to get that.

HOW TO READ ANYONE'S MIND

Advertisement

e world's most successful horse bettor now te

ACCEPT MY "NO-RISK" OFF
PREPARE FOR A MIRAC

...spend your

Advertisement

Advertisement

HOW TO WIN BIG BUCKS AT THE RACETRACK OR OTB!

$000 to $300 a day on the

INTERVIEW WITH MARIE LEWIS

HOW I LOST 39 LBS. IN 29 DAYS

hile I continued eating everything I like!

SO CAN YOU OR MONEY BACK!

e's friends couldn't believe their eyes. People she
seen for awhile almost went into shock and even
she met daily had a problem believing what they
ecause losing 39 pounds in 29 days is no sma
it doesn't go unnoticed when one
of over 1¼lbs. a day!

ed 176 lbs. and
s. In less

Conclusion

In closing, we'll repeat the most important point for you to keep in mind. START SLOWLY — BUT SURELY. Don't do things any faster than you can handle. As is usually true in life, it's better to go step by step. There's absolutely no reason to start with full-page newspaper ads or order an initial 50,000-copy run of your book.

Within a few months, if you've properly handled your initial investments and feel you have a good grip on the market, you can plan bigger ventures.

You can earn so much money with "How To" books, that, once you've gotten your feet wet, you'll find it's worth learning all the angles and keep increasing your knowledge of the field.

I wish you great success, a full letter box every day and the great satisfaction of those who've already employed this method —most of whom have already retired to faraway tropical islands.

Direct marketing allows you to earn money almost immediatly. Customer response is fast. They'll usually contact you within a few days of placing your ad. The money is there. *You're in business.*

Losing Your Hair? Here's How To Keep It A Secret!

...are starting to lose your hair here's
...g exciting you should know about
...easily give you the confidence of
... of hair again.

... is a

...cause your hair

7:20 PM Befor

7:22 PM

How To Create Inner Wea And Become A Milliona

"My life was empty and in financial ruin when I discovered the process of creating inner wealth. As if that was not enough, I found the way to become a millionaire."

...information you are about to read is the
...citing opportunity to build a beautiful life
... that you may ever see.

...ed this very special book which
...ears of research and t...
...and technic...
...life w...

AFTER MY DIS

Life has a fresh an
did not seem to e...

...ich
...v

Examples of a few such books

The following pages list many examples of "How To" books. Each one of them deals with practical sides of life and which will be of interest to a large percentage of the population. The author's name, the publisher's name, the year of publication and the number of pages appear for each of these works. Read the list in full. It is an important source of ideas, and will certainly present some subjects of interest to you. Once you've made your choice(s), you can get copies either of two ways:

(1) By going to the library, you may find the book(s) you've selected. If not, you'll surely find many other books about your selected field. You might also ask the librarian to order them for you, if the library doesn't have them and if he or she finds them interesting.

(2) By going to a bookstore. If they don't have the particular book you've selected, you might still find many other books on the field you've selected. Moreover, the bookstore is quite likely to order the book you want if you give its title, the publishing house, the place and the date of publication and the name of the author.

Bookstores will also have dozens of other "How To" books on hand. They are generally organized alphabetically.

Keep in mind that your first books don't have to be long ones. If they are less than 50 pages, you can sell them for from $4 to $10, depending on the value of the information they contain. Later, after you've gotten together enough money and experience, you can start to write longer books (or even find freelancers who will do the job for you).

So have a good read!

HOW DO YOU FEEL: A GUIDE TO YOUR EMOTIONS
John Wood
Englewood   Cliffs,   N.J.:   Prentice-Hall,   1974,
203 pages

HOW MAIL ORDER FORTUNES ARE MADE
Alfred Stern
Clearwater,   Fla: Selective   Books,   1974,   258
pages

HOW   NEVER   TO   BE   TIRED: OR,   TWO   LIFETIMES   IN
ONE
Marie Beynan Lyons Ray
New   York: Personal   Improvement   Guild,   1944,
339 pages

HOW TO ADVERTISE: A HANDBOOK FOR SMALL BUSINESS
Sandra Linville Dean
Wilmington,   Del,:   Enterprise   Publishing,   1980,
198 pages

HOW   TO   ADVERTISE: CA   PROFESSIONAL   GUIDE   FOR
THE   ADVERTISER.   WHAT   WORKS.   WHAT   DOESN'T   AND
WHY
Kenneth Roman
New York: St.Martin's Press, 1976, 159 pages

HOW TO ADVERTISE AND PROMOTE YOUR SMALL BUSINESS
Gonnie McLung Siegel
New York: J. Wiley, 1978, 128 pages

HOW TO BE A SUCCESSFUL LEADER
Auren Uris
New York: McGraw-Hill, 1953, 339 pages

HOW TO BE HAPPY THOUGH MARRIED
Tim F. Lahaye
Wheaton, Ill.: Tyndale, 1973, 160 pages

HOW TO BE LAZY, HEALTHY AND FIT
Peter Joseph Steincroh
New York: Funk and Wagnalls, 1968, 211 pages

HOW TO BUILD A FORTUNE INVESTING IN LAND
John E. Kirk
Englewood Cliffs, N.J.: Prentice-Hall, 1973,
251 pages

HOW TO BUILD MODERN FURNITURE
Mario Dal Fabbro
New York: F.W. Dodge, 1951, 170 pages

HOW TO BUY: AN INSIDER'S GUIDE TO MAKING MONEY
IN THE STOCK MARKET
Justin Mamis
New York: Farrer, Straus & Giroux, 1982, 245
pages

HOW TO BUY CONDOMINIUM
Patricia Kersen Brooks
New York: Stein and Day, 1975, 191 pages

HOW TO BUY AND MANAGE INCOME PROPERTY
Philip Wik
Englewood Cliffs, N.J.: Prentice-Hall, 1987,
297 pages

HOW TO BUY AND MANAGE RENTAL PROPERTIES
Mike Milin
New York: Simon and Shuster, 1986, 267 pages

HOW TO BUY AND SELL A SMALL BUSINESS
Drake Publishers
New York: Drake Pub., 1975, 122 pages

HOW TO DECORATE AND LIGHT YOUR HOME
E.W. Commery
New York: Coward-McCann, 1955, 256 pages

HOW TO DOUBLE YOUR VOCABULARY
Samuel Stephenson Smith
New YHork: Crowell, 1964, 435 pages

HOW TO EXPLAIN SEX TO CHILDREN
Wayne J. Anderson
New York; the Christophers, 1971, 176 pages

HOW TO FORM YOUR OWN PROFIT/NON PROFIT CORPORATION
WITHOUT A LAWYER
Benji O. Anosike
New York: Do-It-Yourself Legal Publishers, 1981,
128 pages

HOW TO GET A BETTER JOB QUICKER
Richard A. Payne
New York: Taplinger, 1972, 184 pages

HOW TO GET MORE OUT OF SEX: THAN YOU EVER THOUGH
YOU COULD
David R. Reuben
New York: D. McKay, 1974, 299 pages

HOW TO GET STRONG AND HOW TO STAY SO
William Blaikie
S.L.: s.n.

HOW TO GET THE JOB YOU WANT AFTER FORTY
Maxwell J. Harper
New York: Pilot Books, 1967, 80 pages

HOW TO HELP YOURSELF: THE ART OF PROGRAM DEVELOP-
MENT
Robert R. Carkhuff
Amherst, Mass.: Human Resource Development
Press, 1974, 172 pages

HOW TO IMPROVE YOUR PERSONALITY
Roy Newton
New York: Toronto: Gregg Publishing Division,
McGraw-Hill, 1954, 216 pages

HOW TO INVEST FOR BIGGER PROFITS: A PLAIN LANGUAGE
GUIDE TO STOCK MARKET SUCCESS
Charles Warren Goldring
Toronto: MacLean-Hunter, 1957, 80 pages

HOW TO INVEST IN BONDS
Hugh C. Sherwood
New York: Montreal: McGraw-Hill, 1983, 161
pages

HOW TO INVEST IN GOLD STOCKS AND AVOID THE PITFALLS
Donald Hoppe
New Rochelle, N.Y.: Arlington House, 1972,
575 pages

HOW TO INVEST IN MUTUAL FUNDS: FACTS YOU SHOULD
KNOW ABOUT THIS SPECIALIZED FORM OF INVESTING

Amy Margaret Booth

Toronto: MacLean-Hunter, 1964, 56 pages

HOW TO INVEST NOW AND RETIRE RICH
David L. Markstein
New York: Arco, 1973, 87 pages

HOW TO INVEST YHOUR MONEY IN STOCKS AND BONDS:
A SHORT COURSE ON THE INTELLIGENT INVESTMENT
OF PERSONAL FUND IN CANADIAN SECURITIES
Institut canadien des valeurs mobilières
Toronto, 1968, 316 pages

HOW TO INVEST YOUR MONEY AND PROFIT FROM INFLATION
Morton Shulman
New York: Random House, 1980, 165 pages

HOW TO KEEP THE HEART HEALTHY AND FIT
Paul Chappuis Bragg
Burbank: Health Science, 1970, 128 pages

HOW TO LISTEN, HOW TO BE HEARD
Thomas G. Banville
Chicago: Nelson-Hall, 1978, 220 pages

HOW TO LIVE BETTER AFTER 60: A GUIDE TO MONEY,
HEALTH AND HAPPINESS
Robert J. Nissen and Ruth K. Witkin
New York: Regency press, 1978, 280 pages

HOW TO LIVE CHEAP BUT GOOD
Martin Poriss
New York: McGraw-Hill, 1971, 319 pages

HOW TO MAKE LOVE TO THE SAME PERSON FOR THE REST
OF YHOUR LIFE AND STILL LOVE IT
Dagmar O'Connor
New York: Doubleday, 1985, 224 pages

HOW TO MAKE ONE MILLION DOLLARS IN REAL ESTATE
IN THREE YEARS STARTING WITH NO CASH
Tyler Gregory Hicks
Englewood Cliffs, N.J.: Prentice-Hall, 1976,
288 pages

HOW TO MAKE PEOPLE LISTEN TO YOU

Dominick A. Barbara

Springfield, Ill.: C.C. Thomas, 1971, 180 pages

HOW TO MAKE REAL MONEY IN REAL ESTATE
Jack A. Bass
Don Mills, Ont.: Collier Macmillan Canada, 1981,
102 pages

HOW TO MAKE YOUR ADVERTISING TWICE AS EFFECTIVE
AT HALF THE COST
Herschell Gordobn Lewis
Chicago: Nelson-Hall, 1979, 207 pages

HOW TO MAKE YOUR MONEY GROW
Financial Post
Toronto: MacLean-Hunter, 1966, 142 pages

HOW TO NEGOTIATE SUCCESSFULLY IN REAL ESTATE

Tony Hoffman

New York: Simon and Schuster, 1984, 268 pages

HOW TO ORGANIZE YOUR TIME AND RESOURCES
Brian Rothery
London: Business Books, 1972, 106 pages

HOW TO ORGANIZE AND OPERATE A SMALL BUSINESS
Clifford Mason Baumback and Kenneth Lawyer
Englewood Cliffs, N.J.: Prentice-Hall, 1979, 578 pages

HOW TO ORGANIZE MEETINGS: A HANDBOOK FOR BETTER WORKSHNOP, SEMINAR AND CONFERENCE MANAGEMENT
Martin Jones
New York, Toronto: Beaufort Books, 1981, 138 pages

HOW TO PLAY BETTER TENNIS
William Tatem Tilden
New York: Cornerstone Library, 1962, 144 pages

HOW TO PROFIT ON THE REAL ESTATE ROLLER COASTER: AN INVESTOR'S GUIDE TO AVOIDING BIG MISTAKE
Marvin T. Levin
New York: Prentice-Hall, 1986, 205 pages

HOW TO PROSPER IN YOUR OWN BUSINESS: GETTING STARTED AND STAYING ON COURSE

Brian Reffin Smith

Lexington, Mass.: Lewis Publishing, 1981, 323 pages

HOW TO PROTECT AND PATENT YOUR INVENTION: PATENT
LAW
Irving Mandell
Double Ferry, N.Y.: Oceana, 1973, 80 pages

HOW TO PUBLISH YOUR OWN BOOK: A GUIDE FOR AUTHORS
WHO PLAN TO PUBLISH A BOOK AT THEIR OWN EXPENSE
Lothar W. Mueller
Detroit: Harlo Press, 1978, 180 pages

HOW TO READ A PERSON LIKE A BOOK
Gerard I. Nierenberg et Henry H. Calero
New York: Hawthorn Books, 1971, 180 pages

HOW TO READ BETTER AND FASTER
Norman Lewis
New York: Crowell, 1954, 416 pages

HOW TO REALIZE YOUR POTENTIAL
Sheila Hampshire
London: Institute of Personnel Management, 1981,
145 pages

HOW TO REALLY KNOW YOURSELF THROUGH YOUR HANDWRITING
Shirl Solomon
New York: Bantam Books, 1974, 197 pages

HOW TO RETIRE AT FORTY-ONE
L. Rust Hills
Garden City, N.Y.: Doubleday, 1973, 247 pages

HOW TO RIDE AND JUMP YOUR BEST
Barbara Van Tuyl
New York: Grosset and BunLap, 1973, 115 pages

HOW TO RUN A SMALL BUSINESS
J.K. Lasser Tax Institute (New York)
New York, Montréal: McGraw-Hill, 1974, 306 pages

HOW TO RUN A SUCCESSFUL RESTAURANT
William Laird Siegel
New York, Toronto: J. Wiley, 1977, 115 pages

HOW TO SELL ANYTHING TO ANYBODY
Joe Girard
New York: Warner Books, 1981, 191 pages

HOW TO SOLVE YOUR SEX PROBLEMS WITH SELF-HYPNOSIS
Frank Samuel Caprio
North Hollywood, Calif.: Wilshire Book, 1964,
223 pages

HOW TO SPEAK EFFECTIVELY ON ALL OCCASIONS
George Whiting Hibbitt
Garden City, N.Y.: Garden City Books, 1947,
308 pages

HOW TO SPEAK IN PUBLIC
Grenville Kleiser
New York: Funk and Wagnalls, 1912, 533 pages

HOW TO START AND MANAGE YOUR OWN BUSINESS
Gardiner G. Greene
New York, Montréal: McGraw-Hill, 1975, 243 pages

HOW TO START AND OPERATE A MAIL-ORDER BUSINESS
Julian Lincoln Simon
New York: McGraw-Hill, 1976, 462 pages

HOW TO STAR, RUN AND STAY IN BUSINESS
Gregory F. Kishel
New York, Toronto: J. Wiley, 1981, 200 pages

HOW TO START YOUR OWN BUSINESS
William D. Ed Putt
Cambridge, Mass.: Massachusetts Institute of
Technology, 1974, 259 pages

HOW TO START YOUR OWN SMALL BUSINESS
New York: Drake Pub, 1973,

HOW TO STOP HATING AND START LOVING
Jack Birrbaum
London, Angleterre: W. Heinemann, 1975, 194
pages

HOW TO STUDY: TO LEARN BETTER, PASS EXAMINATIONS,
GET BETTER GRADES
Lester Donald Crow, Alice Von Bauer Crow
New York: Collier Books, 1963, 159 pages

HOW TO STUDY
Harry Maddox
London: Pan Books, 1964, 238 pages

HOW TO STUDY

Clifford Thomas Morgan, James Earle Deene
New York: McGraw-Hill, 1957, 130 pages

HOW TO STUDY AND TAKE EXAMS
Lincoln Coles Pettit
New York: J.F. Rider, 1960, 81 pages

HOW TO MAKE BIG MONEY IN THE STOCK MARKET: GOOD
TIMES OR BAD!
David C. Genaway
(Illus.).73p. (Orig.). 1982. pap. 19.95 (ISBN
0-943970-00-8) D C Genaway

HOW TO MAKE BIG MONEY SELLING COMMERCIAL & INDUSTRIAL
PROPERTY
Weldon Girard
1977. 24.95 (ISBN 0-13-417956-0, Busn) P-H

HOW TO MAKE BIG MONEY WITH LITTLE MOVIES
Ivar T. Mattson
LC 78-53375. 1978. pap. 10.00 (ISBN 0-686-13650-0)
PRESCOB

HOW TO MAKE BIG PROFITS FROM LAND IN TRANSITION
Joseph A. Conover
1975. 59.50 (ISBN 0-13-418012-7) Exec Reports

HOW TO MAKE BIG PROFITS RENOVATING REAL ESTATE
Robert P. Gaitens 304 p. 1982. 17.95 (ISBN 0-13-
418103-4) P-H

HOW TO MAKE CANDLES & MONEY
Charles E. Koch
(Illus., Orig.) pap. 2.95 (ISBN 0-87505-226-6) Borden

HOW TO MAKE CHILDREN'S FURNITURE & PLAY EWUIPMENT
Mario Dal Fabbro
2nd ed (Illus.) 192p. 1974 12.95 (ISBN 0-07-015186-5,
P&RB) McGraw

HOW TO MAKE CHRISTMAS ORNAMENTS
Haryette Hendricks
LC 73-79613 (Illus.) 160p. 1973 12.95 (ISBN 0-87294-041-1) Country Beautiful

HOW TO MAKE COLONIAL FURNITURE
F. H. Gottshall
1971 8.95 (ISBN 0-685-01122-4, 80266) Glencoe

HOW TO MAKE COLONIAL FURNITURE
Franklin H. Gottshall
LC 79-20825 1980 17.95 (ISBN 0-02-544840-4) Macmillan

HOW TO MAKE DECISIONS CREATIVELY
John Tobin & Kathleen Feyen
LC 81-80642 160p. (Orig.) 1982 pap. 6.95 (ISBN 0-9605754-0-5) Hartnell Pubns.

HOW TO MAKE DECISIONS THAT PAY OFF
Daniel J. Mathein & Morris B. Squire
LC 81-85832 128p. 1982 pap. write for info. (ISBN 0-931028-28-0) pap. 11.95 (ISBN 0-921028-27-2) Tech'em

HOW TO MAKE DOLLS
N. Edwards
pap. 2.00 (ISBN 0-87497-059-8) Key Bks.

HOW TO MAKE DRAMATIC USE OF WITNESSES TO WIN IN COURT
Charles E. Robbins
1979 69.50 (ISBN 0-13-418194-8) Exec Reports

HOW TO MAKE ELECTRONIC MUSIC
Russell Drake
(Illus.) 1977 pap. 3.95 (ISBN 0-517-52904-1, Harmony) Crown

HOW TO MAKE ESP WORK FOR YOU
Harold Sherman
288p. 1978 pap. 2.75 (ISBN 0-449-23049-X, Crest) Fawcett

HOW TO MAKE FOREIGN DOLLS
Julienne Hallen
pap. 3.00 (ISBN 0-87497-060-1) Key Bks

HOW TO MAKE GROW CLOTHES: FASHIONS THAT GROW WITH
BOYS AND GIRLS
Ruth B. Hinden
(Illus.) 64p. 1981 pap 4.95 (ISBN 0-939842-02-5) RBH Pub.

HOW TO MAKE HANDBAGS
Pier Montagna
pap. 2.00 (ISBN 0-87497-061-X) Key Bks.

HOW TO MAKE HISTORIC AMERICAN COSTUMES
Mary Evans
LC 78-159952 (Illus.) xii, 178p. 1976 Repr. of 1942 ed.
37.00 (ISBN 0-8103-4141-7) Gale

HOW TO MAKE HOME ELECTRICITY FROM WIND WATER & SUNSHINE
John A. Kuecken
(Illus.) 1979 11.95 (ISBN 0-8306-9785-3) pap. 6.95
(ISBN 0-8306-1128-2, 1128) TAB Bks.

HOW TO MAKE IT IN COLLEGE: A SURVIVAL COURSE
Ed. by Hudson Herman 1977 4.00 (ISBN 0-686-18829-2)
Ind U Afro-Amer Arts.

HOW TO MAKE IT THROUGH LAW SCHOOL: A GUIDE FOR
MINORITY & DISADVANTAGED STUDENTS
James P. Davis
150p. 1982 12.95x (ISBN 0-914970-23-2) pap. 5.95
(ISBN 0-686-91875-4) Conch Mag.

HOW TO MAKE KNIVES
Richard W. Barney
Ed. by Wallace BEinfeld 182p. 1977 13.95 (ISBN 0-
917714-13-X BEinfeld Pub.

HOW TO MAKE LAMPSHADES & DRAPERIES
Pier Montagna
pap. 2.00 (ISBN 0-87497-082-2) Key Bks.

HOW TO MAKE LIQUEURS AT HOME
John H. Keers
Jr. 192p. (Orig.) 1973 pap. 1.25 (ISBN 0-532-12174-0)
Woodhill

HOW TO MAKE LOVE TO A MAN
Alexandra Penny
1982 pap. 2.95 (ISBN 0-440-13529-X) Dell.

HOW TO MAKE LOVE TO A MAN
Alexandra Penney
Ed. by Carol Southern 160p. 1981 10.00 (ISBN 0-517-
54145-9, C N Potter) Crown

HOW TO MAKE LOVE TO A SINGLE WOMAN
1977 REpr. of 1975 ed. text ed. 12.95 (ISBN 0-914094-07-6)
Symphony

HOW TO MAKE LOVE TO A WOMAN
Michael Morgenstern
160p. 1982 10.95 (ISBN 0-517-54706-6, C N Potter) Crown

HOW TO MAKE LOVE TO EACH OTHER
Alexandra Penney
1983 10.95 (ISBN 0-399-12743-7) Putnam

HOW TO MAKE LOVE TO YOUR MONEY
Mark Segall & Margaret Tobin
96p. 1982 6.95 (ISBN 0-440-03357-8) Delacorte

HOW TO MAKE A MARRIAGE LAST A LIFETIME
Mary Carson
(Illus. Orig.) 1979 pap. 1.95 (ISBN 0-89570-185-5,
CP-325) Claretian Pubns.

HOW TO MAKE MEETINGS WORK
Michael Doyle & David Straus
320p. 1977 pap. 2.50 (ISBN 0-87216-614-7) Playboy Pbks.

HOW TO MAKE MISSION STYLE LAMPS & SHADES IN METAL & GLASS
rev. ed. Popular Mechanics Co. (Illus.) 128p. Date not set.
pap. 2.95 (ISBN 0-486-24244-7) Dover.

HOW TO MAKE MODEL AIRCRAFT
Chris Ellis
LC 73-92268 (gr. 8 up) 5.95 (ISBN 0-668-03448-3) Arco

HOW TO MAKE MONEY AT HOME WITH THE HELP OF THE UNITED
STATES GOVERNMENT
Ed. by Marshall Bird. (Illus.) 128p. (Orig.) 1980 13.00
(ISBN 0-86567-000-5) Marand Pub Co.

HOW TO MAKE MONEY FAST SPECULATING IN DISTRESSED PROPERTY
John V. Kamin
Ed. by John Kamin 353p. 1983 15.00 (ISBN 0-515-03102-X)
Forecaster Pub.

HOW TO MAKE MONEY FROM ANTIQUES
Mel Lewis
(Illus.) 160p. 1981 12.50 (ISBN 0-7137-1084-5) Pub by
Blandford Pr England) Sterling

HOW TO MAKE MONEY IN ADVERTISING PHOTOGRAPHY
Bill Hammond
(Illus.) 160p. 1975 17.95 (ISBN 0-8174-0581-X) Amphoto

HOW TO MAKE MONEY IN ANTIQUES & COLLECTIBLES BUSINESS
Elyse Sommer
1981 pap. 3.50 (ISBN 0-671-41506-9) PB.

HOW TO MAKE MONEY IN CAKE DECORATING: OWNING & OPERATING
A SUCCESSFUL BUSINESS IN YOUR HOME
Del Carnes
(How to Profit Ser.: Vol. 1, (Illus.) 224p. (Orig.) 1981
pap. 14.95 (ISBN 0-686-30192-7) Deco Pr Pub.

HOW TO MAKE MONEY IN COINS
John V. Kamin
312p. 1976 15.00 (ISBN 0-686-32854-X) Forecaster Pub.

HOW TO MAKE MONEY IN COMMODITIES
Chester W. Keltner
1960 12.50 (ISBN 0-686-00670-4) Keltner

HOW TO MAKE MONEY IN PENNY STOCKS
Jim Scott
LC 81-83125 (Illus.) 96p. 1982 lib. bdg. 14.95 (ISBN
0-915216-85-X) pap. 6.95 (ISBN 0-915216-84-1) Love Street

HOW TO MAKE MONEY IN REAL ESTATE
Steven J. Lee
260p. 1981 50.00 (ISBN 0-932648-19-3) Boardroom

HOW TO MAKE MONEY IN REAL ESTATE
3rd ad. Stanley L. McMichael & Leslie E. Moser
(Illus.) 1968 10.95 (ISBN 0-13-419291-5) P-H

HOW TO MAKE MONEY IN RURAL REAL ESTATE
F. Hathaway
1975 59.50 (ISBN 0-13-419358-X) P-H

HOW TO MAKE MONEY IN THE ANTIQUES-&-COLLECTIBLES BUSINESS
Elyse Sommer
1979 10.95 (ISBN 0-395-27758-2) HM

HOW TO MAKE MONEY IN THE REMODELING BUSINESS
Joseph Berne (Illus.) 1964 11.95 (ISBN 0-8436-0100-0) CBI Pub.

HOW TO MAKE MONEY IN WALL STREET
Louis Rukeyser
LC 73-14055 288p. 1974 7.95 (ISBN 0-385-0750507) pap.
5.95 (ISBN 0-385-04652-9) Doubleday

HOW TO MAKE MONEY IN WALL STREET THROUGH THE INTELLIGENT
USE OF PRICE-EARNINGS RATIOS
Lloyd A. Mitchell
(The New Stock Market Reference Library) (Illus.) 112p.
1981 59.85 (ISBN 0-918968-93-3) Inst Econ Fina

HOW TO MAKE MONEY IN YOUR KITCHEN
Jeffrey Feinman
1977 Morrow

HOW TO MAKE MONEY IN YOUR OWN SMALL BUSINESS
Metcalf et al.
1981 text ed. 16.00(ISBN 0-8359-2965-5) pap. 10.00
(ISBN 0-8359-2964-7) Reston

HOW TO MAKE MONEY IN YOUR OWN SMALL BUSINESS
Wendall O. Metcalf et al.
1977 10.00 (ISBN 0-88205-010-9) pap. 6.95 (ISBN 0-
88205-005-2) Entrepreneur Pr.

HOW TO MAKE MONEY LISTING BUSINESS OPPORTUNITIES
Bertram Klein
1981 9.95 (ISBN 0-533-04710-2) Vantage

HOW TO MAKE MONEY SELLING AT FLEA MARKETS & ANTIQUES FAIRS
rev. ed. Charlotte Harmon
LC 74-14686 (Orig.) 1981 pap. 2.50 (ISBN 0-87576-048-1)
Pilot Bks.

HOW TO MAKE MONEY SPEAKING
Winston K. Pendleton
LC 77-1536 1977 10.00 (ISBN 0-88289-172-3) Pelican

HOW TO MAKE MONEY TRADING LISTED PUTS
Lin Tso
LC 78-9295 182p. 1978 10.95 (ISBN 0-8119-0295-1) Fell

HOW TO MAKE MONEY TWENTY-FOUR HOURS A DAY
Elbert Lee
140p. 1980 pap. 9.95 (ISBN 0-686-28038-5) Positive Pub.

HOW TO MAKE MONEY USING OTHER PEOPLE'S MONEY
Susan Bondy
LC 81-18185 228p. 1982 12.95 (ISBN 0-672-52702-2) Bobbs

HOW TO MAKE MONEY WITH COMPUTERS: A GUIDE TO THIRTY
HIGH-PROFIT, LOW CAPITAL COMPUTER BUSINESS & INVESTMENT
OPPORTUNITIES
Jerry Felsen
LC 78-68050 (Illus.) 1979 20.00 (ISBN 0-916376-05-2)CDS Pub.

HOW TO MAKE MONEY WITH MORTGAGE NOTES
Richard P. Slezer & Wilson Van Dusen
LC 77-92303 (Illus.) 1978 pap. 7.00 (ISBN 0-9601434-1-6)
Philemon Found

HOW TO MAKE MONEY WITH PEN & INK DRAWINGS
Judson Snyder 1981 pap. 3.95 (ISBN 0-918734-30-4) Reymont

HOW TO MAKE MONEY WITH YOUR CAMERA
Ted Schwarz
LC 74-82517 (Illus.) 220p. 1974 pap. 7.95 (ISBN 0-
912656-30-1) H P Bks

HOW TO MAKE MONEY WITH YOUR MICROCOMPUTER
Carl Townsend & Merl Miller
LC 79-53477 1979 pap. 12.95 (ISBN 0-918398-74-6) Dilithium Pr.

HOW TO MAKE MONEY AT INTERIOR DESIGN
Robert Alderman
192p. 1982 18.95 (ISBN 0-442-20876-6) Van Nos Reinhold

HOW TO MAKE MONEY AT INTERIOR DESIGN
Robert Alderman
192p. 1982 write for info. (ISBN 0-442-20876-6) Inter Design

HOW TO MAKE MONEY WITH YOUR GARAGE SALE
Ryan Petty
96p. 1981 pap. 3.95 (ISBN 0-312-39602-3) St Martin

HOW TO MAKE ONE HUNDRED THOUSAND DOLLARS A YEAR SELLING
RESIDENTIAL REAL ESTATE
Dan Ramsey
297p. 1980 14.95 (ISBN 0-13-423582-7, Busn) P-H

HOW TO MAKE ONE MILLION DOLLARS IN REAL ESTATE IN THREE
YEARS STARTING WITH NO CASH
Tyler Hicks
1982 pap. 4.95 (ISBN 0-13-418509-9, Reward) P-H

HOW TO MAKE ONE THOUSAND DOLLARS MONTHLY WITH CLASSIFIED ADS
David Holmes
1978 5.95 (ISBN 0-685-79524-1) Lincoln Pub.

HOW TO MAKE PANTS & JEANS THAT REALLY FIT
Barbara Corrigan
LC 77-74295 (gr. 9 up) 1978 pap. 6.95 (ISBN 0-385-12786-3)
Doubleday

HOW TO MAKE PEOPLE LISTEN TO YOU
Dominick A. Barbara
188p. 1971 photocopy ed. spiral 9.75x (ISBN 0-398-02223-2)
C C Thomas

HOW TO MAKE PLAQUES & MONEY
Charles E. Koch
(Illus., Orig.) pap. 2.00 (ISBN 0-87505-227-4) Borden

HOW TO MAKE POTTERY
Herbert H. Sanders
(Illus.) 144p. 1974 14.50 (ISBN 0-8230-2420-2) Watson-Guptill

HOW TO MAKE TAX-SHELTERED PROFITS FROM INCOME-PRODUCING
REAL ESTATE
Robert S. Schwachter
1980 99.50 (ISBN 0-13-423517-7) Exec Reports

HOW TO MAKE THE BEST OF LIFE
Arnold Bennett
LC 74-5332 (Collected Works of Arnold Bennett: Vol. 33)
1976 Repr. of 1923 ed. 19.75 (ISBN 0-518-19114-1) Arno.

HOW TO MAKE THE MOST OF THE NEW YOU
Linda Fine
LC 80-27861 208p. 1981 11.95 (ISBN 0-668-04919-7) pap. 6.95
(ISBN 0-668-04923-5) Arco.

HOW TO MAKE THINGS GO YOUR WAY
Ralph Charell
192p. 1981 pap. 5.95 (ISBN 0-346-12518-9) Cornerstone

HOW TO MAKE THINGS GROW
David Wickers & John Tuey
(gr. 4-6) 1975 pap. 150 (ISBN 0-590-10136-6, Schol Pap.)
Schol Bk Serv.

HOW TO MAKE WINE IN YOUR OWN KITCHEN
12th ed. Mettja C. Roate (Orig.) 1979 pap.1.75 (ISBN 0-
532-17241-8) Woodhill

HOW TO MAKE WINES & CORDIALS
Andre L. Simon
6.50 (ISBN 0-8446-4604-0) Peter Smith

HOW TO MAKE WIRE JEWELRY
Duane Ferre
(Illus.) 192p. 1980 13.95 (ISBN 0-8019-6859-3) pap.
7.95 (ISBN 0-8019-6860-7) Chilton

HOW TO MAKE YOUR ADVERTISING TWICE AS EFFECTIVE AT HALF
THE COST
H. Gordon Lewis
LC 79-13179 1979 17.95x (ISBN 0-88229-536-5) pap. 19.95x
(ISBN 0-88229-694-9) Nelson-Hall

HOW TO MAKE YOUR CAMERA PAY FOR YOUR VACATION
Frank J. Baker
LC 81-10843 1983 12.95 (ISBN 0-87949-208-2) Ashley Bks.

HOW TO MAKE YOUR CAR HANDLE
Fred Puhn
LC 80-85270 1976 pap. 7.95 (ISBN 0-912656-46-8) H P Bks.

HOW TO MAKE YOUR CAR LAST A LIFETIME
Bob Fendell
LC 80-19759 (Illus.) 216p. 1981 12.95 (ISBN 0-03-053661-8)
pap. 6.95 (ISBN 0-03-053656-1) HR&W

HOW TO MAKE YOUR CHILD A WINNER: TEN KEYS TO REARING
SUCCESSFUL CHILDREN
Victor B. Cline
320p. 1980 14.95 (ISBN 0-8027-0658-4) pap. 9.95 (ISBN 0-
8027-7165-3) Walker & Co.

HOW TO MAKE YOUR DOG AN OBEDIENCE CHAMPION WITHOUT THE
HIGH COST OF AN OBEDIENCE SCHOOL OR TRAINER
Robert J. Kee
(Illus.) 104p. (Orig.) (YA) 1981 pap. 6.00 (ISBN 0-0606370-
0-1, D-B-001) Condor MA

HOW TO MAKE YOUR DREAM WORK FOR YOU
Dian D. Buchman
(gr. 7-12) 1978 pap. 15.0 (ISBN 0-590-11859-5, Schol Pap)
Schol Bk Serv

HOW TO MAKE YOUR DREAMS COME TRUE
Loyd Littlepage
(Illus.) 32p. 1981 pap. 2.50 (ISBN 0-911336-85-0) Sci of Mind

HOW TO MAKE YOUR FIRST QUARTER MILLION IN REAL ESTATE IN
FIVE YEARS
Dan Ramsey
1980 10.95 (ISBN 0-13-418350-9) P-H

HOW TO MAKE YOUR FIRST QUARTER MILLION IN REAL ESTATE IN
FIVE YEARS
Dan Ramsey
1982 pap. 4.95 (ISBN 0-13-418343-6, Reward) P-H

HOW TO MAKE YOUR INFORMATION WORK FOR YOU
Sherril Kennedy & Marcia Purnell
1981 29.95x (ISBN 0-86176-03306, Pub. by MCB Pubns)
State Mutual Bk.

SAMPLE ADVERTISEMENTS

40 sample advertisements for "How To" books follow.

It's not necessary for you to read them all in full. But glance at them, at least. Examine how they're laid out and take note of any photos or graphic work they contain.

Remember — your first ads don't have to be full-page spreads. Start by writing short ads. In the beginning, there are many advantages to do things this way:

(1) They are easier to write and require less work.

(2) Ads with little text can be laid out in smaller spaces: 1/20, 1/10, 1/8, 1/6 or 1/4 of a page. Bear in mind that a 1/8-page ad costs about 1/8 as much as a full page ad and 1/16 what a two-page spread does. This might seem obvious, but taking such a precaution often represents the difference between those who succeed because they are careful and those who fail because of excess confidence in their advertising. Always test your advertising in low-circulation newspapers to start.

Subsequently — once you've written many ads and have more experience — you can start writing lengthier copy and pay for larger ads in papers with bigger circulations.

How and Where to Get Good Paying Career Oriented, College Jobs

by Edward Rosenwasser

A brief, but thorough guide to jobs that, as author Edward Rosenwasser says, contribute to gains in maturity, motivation, academic performance, self-reliance...and the list goes on. Find out how classroom education can be combined with related work experience. Rossenwasser lists the various colleges (community, four-year and graduate) that offer specific jobs relating to a student's field of study. An excellent opportunity is available for those who want to earn money, learn job skills, and have a foot up on other students upon graduation.

1782 $10.00

How and Why to Incorporate

by Willian Headrick

Along with the prestige of being in charge of your own corporation, incorporation can provide you and your company with many tax breaks. Incorporation may also reduce your liabilities, which may mean further savings for you. This concise booklet tells you what a corporation is and how it is formed. Additionally, chapters tell you how to go about incorporating, and what your rights and obligations are. A second part of the guide tells you how your newly formed corporation can open up new opportunities for you, including valuable tax savings. Find out all the benefits of incorporating in this handy guide.

How to Achieve Total Success

by Russ von Hoelscher

More than just telling you how to achieve financial success, this book tells you how to get anything you want — in short, how to be totally successful. This book will help you multiply your own power, so nothing can stand in your way; this book "will take you from where you are now to where you want to be."

(9½ x 6½) #0933; $15.00

How to Avoid 22 Costly Mistakes in Mail Order

by Jerry Buchanan

Often a beginner in the mail order will make costly mistakes, mistakes so costly that they may mean the difference between rags and riches. Jerry Buchanan has identified 22 of these mistakes, and tells you how to avoid them. By following his advice you can be more discriminating, more professional and more successful. This is for you if your thinking of becoming involved in mail order, are or if you are already involved and want to be more successful.

1759 $14.95

How to Become a Successful Freelance Writer

by Jordan R. Young

Jordan Young has written over 300 articles, including articles for many of this country's top newspapers and other nationally known publications. Here he offers some of the secrets he has learned through experience as a successful freelance writer. The complete process to getting your writings published are presented: from 'queries' to writing on 'spec.' Included is a glossary of terms every freelance writer should know. Also included are ideas on where you should get published, along with protecting your interests, so you get the maximum profit from your writings.

1761 $12.00

Advertisement

How To Collect Social Security At Any Age

(*Special*) A new book written by a former Federal investigator tells how every American can collect their share of the $250 billion that will be handed out this year by Uncle Sam. The book explains how to collect: social security before retirement, small business loans, income supplements, education benefits, farm loans, unemployment, job training, even welfare and food stamps. Here are just a few facts covered:

• How 37 million Americans, averaging around age 30, collect monthly social security checks.

• How to make the entire family eligible for social security, even your youngest child.

• How you may be cheating yourself out of social security benefits.

• How almost 3 million childen get monthly social security checks.

• How to qualify for disability pensions (over 3.5 million people collecting but thousands more eligible).

• How to work and still collect social security.

• How to find out how much you have paid into Social Security.

• How to know when to quit work and start collecting social security.

• How to get a lump sum payment.

• How to get a $500,000 loan to start your own business. (It's simple and the book tells you exactly how to do it).

• How to collect a $250,000 loan to buy a farm or ranch, including livestock and equipment.

• How to collect a $27,000 loan for a mobile home, including lot.

• How to collect a $15,000 loan for home improvements.

• How to collect over $400 a month to attend college, trade school or get on-the-job training.

• How to get free medical coverage, including eye glasses and dental care.

• How to get a good-paying Federal job.

• How to collect hundreds of dollars a month to pay your apartment rent, including utilities.

• How to get up to a $100,000 small business loan, even if you are poor and unemployed.

• How to obtain thousands of dollars in free Federal services.

With the help of this book, many families are now leading a more comfortable existence.

Although the book "How To Collect Big Dollars From Uncle Sam" could mean thousands of dollars to you, it is being offered at only $12.95 (plus $1 post. & hldg).

Order from: R. Emil Neuman

You can return the book within 30 days if not 100% satisfied and receive a full refund.

How To Borrow Your Way To Real Estate Riches

by Tyler Hicks

With little or no money of your own, and with no special real estate training, you can start right not to take advantage of this dnyamic income-producing system to build a quick fortune in real estate. Backed up with dozens of real-estate examples, this extraordinary guide reveals the "insider" techniques for getting the financing that you need to acquire valuable real estate. Tyler Hicks will show you how to make all of this possible.
#3855 $10.00

How to Get Any Credit Card You Want, Even If You Have Bad Credit

by Joseph Wright

Time to get out of the "credit hole" and create a new life for yourself. This book tell you what your credit reputation is, how it is determined and how knowing all this information will aid in controlling your credit destiny. You find out how to put your feet on the road to good credit. Included is a complete, systemized approach to getting that good credit. Also contains a comprehensive list of low-interest credit cards available nationwide. Take that first step to creating a new life of credit for YOU!
#9937; $15

How To Get Anything You Want Absolutely Free Or Next To Nothing

by Phil Williams

Find out how to find those elusive bargains and get products for free in this new book. Learn how to get bargains at closeouts, get government surplus, get goods for 10 cents on the dollar and many other bargains that seem too good to be true.
#4733; $10

How to Get Rich in Mail Order

by Melvin Powers

You can learn what to do and what not to do in starting your own mail order business from the voice of experience— Melvin Powers, a book publisher and mail order entrepeneur, who has worked in this profitable business for over 25 years. In this volume he shares what he has learned and can help make you successful in this field. Powers shows you how to be creative and, thus, profitable. This book shows you strategies for success, along with practical advice on marketing, advertising and finding a product and service to sell. It is full of samples and examples, so it is easy to learn from this book. Additionally, the book tells you how to sell products on television. The variety of subjects covered makes this a valuable reference source for the person interested in the mail order business.

2655 $20.00

How to Get Rich in Multilevel Marketing

by David Holmes & Joel Andrews

You can get rich without working by using the multi-level approach. Your agents get the product from the company, but you get the commission from your agents and each agent they enlist. Others do the work while you sit back and collect the high commissions. Thousands of people just like you are making more than $100,000 a year without working. Once you have this book you can begin to create your fortune with any product you choose. Holmes and Andrews have combined 20 years of sales and marketing experience. Holmes, a marketing expert and author of two books, has made more than 150 television and radio appearances over the past year. Andrews, who has personally launched six successful business ventures, is so highly regarded in sales and marketing that he has testified on marketing to both houses of Congress. Together, these men teach you how to get rich without working.

1855 $14.95

How to Get Rich with Your Microcomputer

by Edwin Simpson

The ongoing computer explosion has made the computer affordable to everyone. Now you can take the computer and put it to work to make you money. HOW TO GET RICH WITH YOUR MICRO-COMPUTER gives the hopeful computer entrepeneur suggestions on how to grow. Suggestions on computer-related enterprises and how to profit on them are given, along with a business primer and advertising suggestions. Even the beginner with a computer can put this book to use to make money with an inexpensive computer. Suggested businesses and thorough explanations ensure that with this book and a computer, you can't lose.

1730 $12.00

How to Make a Fortune Writing and Selling Information by Mail

by David Buckley

This manual by David Buckley tells you how to get into the mail order business. His tips and secrets make it plain how easy it is to make money from writing information. Never written before? This book shows how easy it really is. Don't know what kind of books will sell? This book reveals what types of information will do well. Not sure how selling by mail works? This manual will reveal all you need to know. Short on funds? This book shows you how to minimize your expenses, while greatly expanding your profits. It's amazing how valuable information can be, and how you can profit on its worth. And when you have someone as experienced as David Buckley as a guide, then you will be on the "write" track to making your fortune through selling information by mail.

3533 $10.00

How to Make Money Writing and Selling Simple Information

by J.E. Barnes

Everybody has a book inside them; some information that they know they can share with the rest of the world and that, at the same time, can make them money. But it always seems some obstacles stop people from achieving this dream. Well no longer! J.E. Barnes shows you how to write, publish and sell information. Even if you don't have an idea right now, don't worry, Barnes offers hundreds of examples that you can use. This book is so complete that it takes you through the steps of writing (no, you don't need to be a Hemingway to make money), publishing, copywriting without a lawyer, setting up a business, selling your books, and, best of all, how to have fun doing it. It really isn't complicated or hard to get that book you have within you into the hands of readers if you follow the ideas presented in HOW TO MAKE MONEY WRITING AND SELLING SIMPLE INFORMATION.

0317   ━━━━━━━ $15 00

How to Obtain Maximum College Financial Aid

by Edward Rosenwasser

No matter what age you are, whether you are already in college or are considering going, you don't need to let financial need stand in the way of your education. Edward Rosenwasser gives you a complete guide that cuts through the 'fog' surrounding college aid. He tells you what's available and what you need to do to get it. He offers you clear facts and figures to explain how college financial aid works and how to maximize the amount of aid with the minimum time and cost. Additionally, he offers you names and addresses of government and private scholarships and loans, so you can get the ball rolling right away.

1781 $10.00

How to Publish Your Own Book Successfully

by Lee Howard

'This manual contains the complete facts that enable you to publish books, booklets, directories, etc., successfully.' In this handy manual you will get the complete facts on putting out your own book, and how to capitalize on it by making money. Learn case histories of successful small publishers; find out how to get started; discover how to sell books by mail. Included is valuable advice on getting money to publish your book, on keeping your costs low and on getting publicity to maximize your returns; this and much more practical advice in one handy manual. This useful guide has complete sources for everything you need to be a publisher.

1723 $10.00

How To Turn Your Bad Debt Into AAA-1 Credit

by Joseph Wright

You can get out of debt forever and receive AAA-1 credit! This exciting book tells you how to erase bad debt and get an SBA loan. You'll learn about personal and debt loan companies, venture capital and minority business development agencies. Do you know what an SBIC is? I tell you how SBIC can help you. Includes information on the General Services Administration regional offices and lists other important agencies. This book is a "must have" if you want out of debt!

#9935; $15

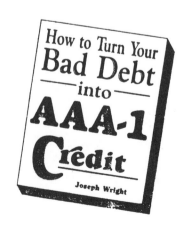

How to Sell Books by Mail
by Joseph Soukup

Everyone reads, so there's always a constant demand for books of all kind. So why not tap this well of riches by selling books by mail? Here is a successful plan of action to teach you how to take advantage of this field, from the ground up. The advice is practical and sound telling you the ins and outs so you won't be left in the dark. Among the valuable suggestions are those on the various business aspects of selling books by mail. Included is the directory of wholesale book sources, listing addresses and prices on wholesale books, so you'll even have valuable contacts before you start into this business!

1562 $8.95

How To Think Small Business For Big Profits
By Reynold Jay

HOW TO THINK SMALL BUSINESS FOR **BIG PROFITS**

Every small business has the potential to earn big profits for its owner If you are thinking about going into business or are just starting out, this information is essential if you are to succeed!

This exciting book shows you step by step how to start up your business on a shoestring budget and propel yourself to incredible wealth.

It is presented in simple clear language.

Some of the features in this 8½ x 11, 40,000 word, 106 page book.

- **Discover the 12 common mistakes** of small business owners and how to avoid them.

- **How to start** your business from your home.

- **Take the 12 tough question test** in order to see if you have the guts to make it is small business.

- **Discover the five basic attributes** of every self-made millionaire.

- **Learn how to advertise** effectively. Obtain free advertising. Advertise in a cost effective manner.

- **Learn the nuts and bolts** of setting up your business.

COMMENTS FROM READERS
"Takes the mystery out of starting a business." - Salesman.
"It's given me new direction." - Musician

IRON CLAD GUARANTEE. If you are not completely satisfied with the book after ten days you may return it for a full refund.

Just complete the coupon below and your book will be sent promptly to you.

To: C. W. Publishing

Please send me
_____ copies of "HOW TO THINK SMALL BUSINESSES FOR BIG PROFITS" at $9.95 each plus $2.00 postage and handling.
_____ 1 hr. cassette(s), Pt. 1 at $9.95 ⁴ .85 shipping.
_____ 1 hr. cassette(s), Pt. 2 at $9.95 ⁴ .85 shipping.
☐ check enclosed   ☐ money order enclosed
Name (Please print) _____
Address _____
City _____ State ____ Zip _____
Add enough to cover ship. for spec. del., foreign, air, etc.

©1987 Confectionery Word Inc.

How to Use Your Hidden Potential to Get Rich

by David Bendah

This book presents a program that clearly maps the route self-made millionaires took to make their fortunes. Any very successful person who has made millions has used the techniques in this book. Hidden Potential will show any individual, regardless of skill, intelligence and experience, how to use the mind to realize both business and personal dreams. A complete success program, it is illustrated with charts and diagrams that enable understanding of the mind-transformation process. Included are quizzes that monitor the reader's progress to wealth. David Bendah backs up his points with interesting examples of how ordinary people used the sample techniques to make fortunes. Bendah also devotes three chapters to Japanese wealth-building techniques. In short, this volume is designed to expose the reader to every success principle needed to get rich.

0433 $12.00

MAKE YOUR CLASSIFIED AD PAY
Get "How to Write a Classified Ad That Pulls." Includes Certificate worth $2.00 towards a classified ad in this publication. Send $3.25 to Davis Publications, Inc., Dept. CL,

How to Write a Good Advertisement

by Victor Schwab

The more books on advertising you study, the better you will be at writing ads. One especially recommended book is *How to Write a Good Advertisement*, a *Short Course on Copywriting*, by Victor O. Schwab, one of the best copywriters of this century. He created many famous ads—one, for *How to Win Friends and Influence People*, sold 5 million copies for author Dale Carnegie. Schwab's techniques are continuously studied by the top advertising agencies, and you should study them, too. Instead of focusing on the structure of the successful ad, Schwab concentrates on the psychology of the consumer.

1455 $15.00

How You Can Make a Fortune Selling Information by Mail

by Russ von Hoelscher

Full time or spare time, the money-making potential of mail order information marketing is tremendous. In this remarkable new book, Russ von Hoelscher, the grand master of mail order and information sales, shows you how to make a fortune in this most rewarding business.

Just a partial list of contents:
- How to find saleable "information" products
- The secrets of gettin grich with "paper & ink"
- How to self-publish your own books, manuals, directories, reports, newsletters, tapes, etc., even if you have no previous writing or publishing experience.
- How to launch your business with very little investment
- Why "specialized" information is the key to riches
- Space advertising—how to use it to become rich
- How to make big money with direct mail
- Russ von Hoelscher's master marketing techniques
- How famous writer/publisher Melvin Powers has sold over 200,000,000 books—most of them by mail.
- What the legendary Joe Karbo told Russ about creative marketing
- How to obtain free advertising and publicity, and more.

9408 $15.00

Your Nerves Can Heal Themselves

Dr.
Patrick
Quillin

(SPECIAL)—If you've been feeling nervous, tense or irritable lately, doctors have discovered it may be because of improper brain nutrition.

Your brain needs the right balance of 52 essential nutrients to function properly, reveals Dr. Patrick Quillin in his vital new health guide "How to Make Your Nerves Heal Themselves." Without knowing it, you could have one or more nutritional deficiencies that may lead to anxiety, irritability, depression, mood swings, forgetfulness, foggy thinking, and a host of other symptoms commonly referred to as "nerves."

Dr. Quillin is a nationally respected nutrition expert and former health consultant to the United States Government. "How to Make Your Nerves Heal Themselves" explains how you, simply by eating the right combination of foods, can release your body's natural nerve calmers and healers. You can actually begin to feel results in a remarkably short period of time. Dr. Quillin's work is thoroughly researched and medically endorsed. This indispensable aid to better health reveals:
- **Which nutrients are natural nerve calmers**
- **Which diet factors reduce anxiety and depression**
- **Which deficiencies can cause irritability and which can correct it**
- **Which foods may reduce some of the symptoms of Alzheimer's disease**
- **Which deficiencies can lead to premature destruction of brain tissue**
- **Which diet factors may improve the shakes commonly associated with aging**
- **Which supplements may improve memory**
- **Which supplements your brain needs to function at peak efficiency**
- **Which nutrients enhance alertness and help you think more clearly**

- **How prescription drugs affect brain nutrition**

"How to Make Your Nerves Heal Themselves" can help you feel more relaxed, more at ease and more in control. It can help you feel more confident and better able to cope with the day to day pressures of modern life. It can help you feel like you have a new lease on life. You'll learn more vital health-saving information, such as:
- **10 different vitamins older adults are lacking**
- **How to reduce fatigue**
- **How to improve blurred vision**
- **Which helper nutrients your body needs to get the most out of the foods you eat**
- **Which nutrients may help slow some of the symptoms of aging**
- **How to encourage normal, healthy sleep**
- **Which diet factors increase oxygen to the brain**
- **Which mineral deficiencies can lead to poor judgment and even high blood pressure**
- **Which foods can trigger migraine headaches**
- **How to protect yourself against pollution and commercial food additives**
- **Which foods seem to create more infections**
- **And much, much more**

"How to Make Your Nerves Heal Themselves" is not available in bookstores. Right now it is available to readers of the Globe/Examiner as part of a special press run. Your satisfaction is 100% guaranteed. If you are dissatisfied in any way, simply return it in 30 days for a full refund—no questions asked.

To order, simply print your name and address and the words "Heal Nerves" on a piece of paper and mail it along with cash, check or money order for just $8.95 plus $1.00 postage and handling. ($9.95 total.) Mail to: THE LEADER CO., INC., Publishing Division.

VISA or MasterCard, send card number and expiration date. Act now. Orders will be fulfilled on a first-come, first-served basis.

© 1989 The Leader Co., Inc.

YOU CAN EASILY MAKE A SUCCESS IN THE MAIL ORDER WORLD

Yes, if you have a product or invention learn how to sell it by mail. If you don't have a product this book will show you how to get one. PLUS, it will explore the 24 major mail order markets so you can select the best one for you.

START on a shoestring if you wish. Build a business that will pay you an income for the rest of your life. Remember, a mail order business can be operated from any location . . . any state . . . city or even rural area.

START OFF RIGHT . . . Don't flounder around for years trying to find the right way to operate. Learn the facts, now, right at the start. SAVE MONEY by using it wisely and correctly. Thousands may start a mail order business, lose a little money and then drop out, never really knowing what it was all about. Don't make that mistake. Before you start, read this book, let it show you step by step everything you need to know.

PART TIME OR FULL TIME . . . Businessman, salesman, employee, retired, housewife . . . earn spare time or full time dollars . . . Mail Order can be for you!

Do you want a Mail Order business paying you $25,000, $50,000 or even $100,000 a year. Many are doing just that with their own independent Mail Order business.

SUCCESS STORIES ABOUND . . . Look through your magazines and newspapers at the mail order ads. Many of these people have been advertising year in and year out for 10, 20, 30 or more years. Are they successful? You bet they are. Of course some people may think of Sears Roebuck when they think of mail order, but there are thousands of smaller one-man businesses specializing in just one or a few products. The possibilities in mail order are fantastic. The post office helps you to reach your customers. READ THE SUCCESS STORIES IN "HOW MAIL ORDER FORTUNES ARE MADE."

CAN YOU MAKE MONEY IN THE MAIL ORDER BUSINESS? If you are able to read and follow directions, the answer is YES!
Here in easy to understand language is the whole procedure for beginning and continuing a successful mail order business, written by an expert who knows the business.

No expensive rent to pay . . . none of the problems of the retail store . . . in fact with a mail order business you can take off for a vacation whenever you want . . . work only 3 or 4 days a week. Set your own schedule. Live like you have always wanted to live.

IT'S EASY when you know how.

NEVER BEFORE has there been a book with the HOW TO DO IT facts and figures. Others have paid hundreds of dollars for seminars or private consultations to get the facts and ideas that you can get in this book.

FULLY ILLUSTRATED. Dozens of actual successful mail order ads are shown in this book. Specific sales letters that have been successfully used are shown. The factual statements are fully backed up with illustrations and examples.

EASY TO UNDERSTAND . . . written in simple everyday language so that even if you are inexperienced in business you can easily grasp the fundamental points. Mail Order teminology is completely explained.

NEW, REVISED, and UPDATED Edition now available. This best-selling book is now in its 5th printing. It has been updated to reflect current marketing trends and the most up-to-date principles of mail order marketing.

The World of Mail Order Selling . . . They Struck it Rich . . . Capital Required . . . How to Get Started . . . Names . . . 7 Approaches . . . Find Products . . . What Price Products . . . Good M.O. Products . . . Direct Mail vs. Publication Ads . . . Mailing Lists . . . Classified/Display Ads . . . Making Classified Ads Pay . . . The Market is Big . . . Women's—Men's—Youth Market . . . Beauty . . . Baby . . . Gift-Giving . . . Jewelry . . . Sell Courses . . . Books . . . Health Products . . . Stamps, Coins . . . Food . . . Records . . . The Farmer . . . Premiums . . . Sell Dealers . . . Off-Beat Items . . . Fads & Gags . . . Special Angles . . . Tricks & Gadgets . . . Preparing Ads . . . Words that Pull . . . Copy . . . Layout . . . Order Forms . . . Testimonials . . . Sales Letters . . . Coupons . . . Timing . . . Record Systems . . . Radio/TV . . . Catalog Houses . . . Mail Order Houses . . . Publicity (How to get it) . . . Trade Magazines . . . PLUS much much more . . . 79 sections.

HERE, ALL IN ONE BOOK is the information that you might take years to discover on your own. The facts in this book are worth over $1,000 to the person who sincerely wants to make his fortune, large, or small, in the MAIL ORDER BUSINESS.

THE AUTHOR takes you by the hand through every facet of the MAIL ORDER BUSINESS . . . gives illustrations of what others have done . . . tells you what you can do . . . IF YOU WANT TO EARN A large 5 figure income in your spare time . . . READ THIS BOOK . . . the MAIL ORDER BUSINESS IS YOUR OPPORTUNITY! . . . LIMITLESS OPPORTUNITY . . . there are so many new products . . . so many items that people need that there is room for everyone that wants to be in the mail order business . . . FASCINATING AND PROFITABLE . . . There's nothing like having money roll out of envelopes addressed to you. GET STARTED NOW . . . let Alfred Stern take you through the pages of this book on your way to your own MAIL ORDER BUSINESS.

ALFRED STERN, AUTHOR is a successful Account Executive in N.Y.C. specializing in Mail Order for a quarter of a century. Here is what some clients have had to say about him:

"You are wonderful Mr. Stern! Thanks a lot for all your help." Calif. . . . "You have done a tremendous job and I am really convinced that you know what you are doing." New York . . . "You have been a tremendous help in getting me off on the right foot in the mail order business and I do appreciate it." Illinois . . . Alfred Stern is one of the best, most reliable and extremely devoted mail order men in the U.S. Pioneer Press, Tenn.

Mail Today To: National Paperback Books, Inc

Enclosed is my: [ ] check; [ ] Money order   for $9.99
I understand that I have a full thirty days to examine my book and may return it for an unconditional refund if I'm not completely satisfied.

Add $1 per book for shipping & handling
TN residents add 7% sales tax   #584

Name _____

Address _____

City _____ State _____ Zip Code _____

POWER

THESE TOTAL SUCCESS MIND-SCIENCE *"MASTERY OF LIFE"* STRATEGIES AND TECHNIQUES GIVE YOU THE POWER TO SUCCEED!

UNLOCK YOUR POWER FORCE

Hidden in the deep recesses of your mind is an awesome source of power that can quickly transform your life and bring you everything you want. This amazing Force is within all, but only a few are consciously aware of it and know how to use it. The new mastery of life manual, *HOW TO ACHIEVE TOTAL SUCCESS* clearly explains what IT is, how it works and how you can use it. *You will discover and master simple, yet extremely effective Mind Science methods that allow you to control and direct your goals and make your life a rich, romantic, and rewarding experience.* This incredible success program by Russ von Hoelscher can positively change your life forever.

ERASE THE FEARS THAT CONTROL AND BIND YOU

HOW TO ACHIEVE TOTAL SUCCESS gives you 442 pages of amazing mind-science techniques that allow you to control your life, and everything in it. This is vital knowledge for any person who wants to "get high on life, and live the life that is free, rich, whole, healthy and happy. Now you do not have to settle for less. *You can have it all!* The mind-science success principles will erase fear, doubt and the subconscious negative programing that has restricted you.

NOTHING IS IMPOSSIBLE

HOW TO ACHIEVE TOTAL SUCCESS is truly a miracle-multiplying success course, all in one huge, 442-page volume. You can't miss if you will work with this! Russ von Hoelscher offers all the tools that will make you successful. Topics include:

Goal achieving made easy; the dynamics of Scientific Affirmations that will deliver the results you desire; Creative Visualization— how to remake your world exactly the way you want it; the secret power of a Success Covenant—divine partnership with The Source; Metaphysical prayer and meditation that will maintain or restore good health, Mind-Science and money—wealth-building techniques that create riches; the amazing power of Unconditional Love; the truth about sexual energy, a guide to satisfying relationships, PLUS MUCH MORE!

This huge, practical "positive life-book" also includes an A TO Z guide to Total Success which covers most of life's little dramas and big challenges. Complete with the proven "Mind Science Principles" that guarantee you will overcome, take control, and enjoy the total experience.

100,000 LIVES ENRICHED!

Over one hundred thousand people worldwide have already experienced the power of *Total Success.*

Here's what some of them are saying:

"From deep depression, loss of my husband and my job, and having serious thoughts of committing suicide, to success, money and love, sweet love! I thank God for what How to Achieve Total Success has done for me."
Name withheld
by request
Boca Raton, FL

"I've never seen anything like it. Total Success is a miracle! It has helped me turn my life completely around. My new business is prospering and I'm engaged to be married to the sweetest girl in the world."
J.B. Miller, Jr.
Indianapolis, IN

"How to Achieve Total Success has changed my life. More money, satisfaction, power and happiness are now mine! Thanks a million, Russ."
Cal Kern
Houston, TX

"This powerful, enlightened manual has made a great impact on my life. I've rediscovered the joy of living. Enclosed is my order for 50 more copies so that I may share this incredible experience with friends, clients and loved ones."
Dr. T.R.C.
Buffalo, NY

"Magnificent and very motivational..."
Howard Jan
author of THE
SUCCESS JOURNAL

"This book is remarkable. Truly, a great, achievement."
Mayor Steve Lockman
Lancaster, MN

"A beautiful, inspiring book..."
Dottie Walters
Author & famous
professional speaker

▶ FREE BONUS

PRESCRIPTIONS FOR HAPPINESS, the beautiful, simple and very practical new book by Ken Keyes, Jr. (author of the best-selling *Handbook to Higher Consciousness*) is included in its entirety as part of the *HOW TO ACHIEVE TOTAL SUCCESS,* mastery of life edition.

Send for *HOW TO ACHIEVE TOTAL SUCCESS* today! It will open your heart to unconditional love, your mind to new awareness, your body to better health and your finances to ever-increasing wealth. Say *"YES"* to your success!

"Fantastic! Total Success can help anyone achieve great success."
Robert J. Sturner
Leading motivator and
founder of Super Life

"Congratulations! How to Achieve Total Success is interesting, innovative and helpful."
Norman Vincent Peale
World-famous author

What Total Success has done for others— it will do for you!

WHAT IS TOTAL SUCCESS?

It's feeling good about yourself and knowing how to use the incredible Power Source you have within you. This total Power Force can and will bring you everything you want and need. You need only know how to channel this power in your life. *HOW TO ACHIEVE TOTAL SUCCESS* shows you how to do it!

Total Success gives you the power of choice. The ability to choose and attract the persons and conditions you want to share your love and experiences with. *Total Success* includes enjoying excellent health in body, mind and emotions. It's having enough money to live comfortably and the ability to be very rich, if that is your desire. Above all, *Total Success* is loving yourself and others enough to allow yourself to be happy most of the time in spite of it all—and *because* of it all!

ORDER FORM

National Paperback Books, Inc

YES! Enclosed find $12.95 plus $1 postage/handling—total $13.95. Rush me my copy of the 442-pg. edition of *HOW TO ACHIEVE TOTAL SUCCESS* by Russ von Hoelscher.
Enclosed find: ☐ Check ☐ Money Order
Tennessee residents add 7% tax.

Card No._____ Exp._____

Signature _____

Name _____

Address _____

City, State, Zip _____

HOW TO BECOME A BUSINESS TYCOON

Have You Ever Dreamed of Owning
YOUR OWN BUSINESS ...
But Thought You Could Not Afford It?

THINK AGAIN FRIEND!

For Now, For the First Time Ever, All the
Tricks and Secrets To the Art of Acquiring
Your Own Business(s) With *Little Or
Nothing Down* Are Revealed

HOW TO BE A
'BUSINESS TYCOON'
THE ART OF BUYING BUSINESSES WITH LITTLE OR
NOTHING DOWN...EVEN IF YOU'RE FLAT BROKE

by SAM I PARADICE

Revealed in Sam Paradice's Latest Book ... HOW TO BECOME A BUSINESS TYCOON!

NO ORDINARY BOOK

Mr. Paradice's experience and expertise uniquely qualify him to lecture nationwide on the subject of little or no money down business purchases.

As a business and real estate entreprenuer, Sam Paradice has bought and sold millions of dollars worth of business ownership and property. He personally has used many of the techniques he describes in this unique book and seen the others in action. His hands on experience means better, more practical advice and information for you. No classroom or book learner, Sam Paradice can lecture from real-life, day-to-day experiences.

HERE'S SOME OF WHAT YOU'LL LEARN ... JUST FOR STARTERS

• Learn over sixty-five different methods to buy a business with little or nothing down!
• Learn how it is possible to buy a business even with little or no credit!
• Discover how to prepare a nothing down purchase offer!
• Learn how to find the right business!
• Learn how to get a co-signer for a business loan!
• Discover how to use the "domino" method of buying multi-unit businesses!
• Little known technique revealed that will let you start your own auto dealership with none of your own money!
• Learn about a business club you can join that offers business financing ... $1,000-$5,000 with no collateral required, no co-signers and no credit check!

Other books by financial wizard
Sam Paradice

*The Arab Money Hotline
Free Money
Real Estate Counterattack
Payday*

• Learn how to start your own private international bank!
• Discover how to form your own public corporation for a fraction of the cost an underwriter would charge you!
• Learn how to evaluate the potential of a business for sale. Avoid common mistakes that beginners make!
• Learn how to determine the current value of a business!
• Learn how to buy a business without buying the business!
• Learn how to buy a business using the sellers cash!
• And so, so much more!

OVER 65 DIFFERENT METHODS TO BUY A BUSINESS WITH LITTLE OR NOTHING DOWN

Not just a list of financing techniques, but a high-powered, frank discussion of each technique, its advantages and pitfalls.

Plus dozens of other tidbits to help you better understand financing and improve your bank balance!

NO HOLDS BARRED

Mr. Paradice tells it like it is. He speaks from your perspective, but informs you what others like the sellers and bankers will see. He shows you how to buy businesses on a friendly basis and how to be UTTERLY RUTHLESS.

YOU CAN BE A TYCOON!

Imagine yourself as the boss. Imagine yourself at the helm of your own business. You making the decisions. Giving yourself the raise you deserve. Hiring and firing whom you please. Hobnobbing with other business and civic leaders in your community.

Who says you can't afford it. We say you can do it with a lot less than you think ... even no money down! Order this dynamic book today. Study it carefully ... then step out and purchase your own business!

GUARANTEE

Our guarantee is simple, and it's all in your favor. If you don't like your copy of "How To Become A Business Tycoon" for any reason whatever, just return it to us. We'll send your fifteen dollars back the same day ... no questions asked. You must be satisfied that this book is all we say it is or your money back!

Clip the coupon below   National Paperback Books, Inc
and order today from:

YES! I want to become a BUSINESS TYCOON! Rush my copy of the Paradice creative wealth course, "HOW TO BECOME A BUSINESS TYCOON"
#1790

I understand that I must be satisfied that this course can do all you say and more or I get my money back! If I do elect to return the course, you will refund my money in full within 24 hours. I can take a full thirty days to review my book under your guarantee.

Enclosed is my payment of $15.00 in ☐ Check ☐ Money order
Tennessee residents add 7% sales tax./Add $1 per book for shipping & handling.

NAME _____

ADDRESS _____

CITY _____ STATE _____ ZIP _____

How To CASH IN BIG WITH REFUNDS & COUPONS

In a recent year, coupon discounts alone saved the American shopper about $561 million dollars! And this doesn't include refund offers! Even though these figures sound impressive....under 5% of the total coupons distributed were redeemed!

Are you one of the persons that runs to the supermarket and pays full price? By using the weekly grocery special sale items and redeeming cash-off coupons, you could save from 10%-15% the first week! By adding in refund activities, you could up your total savings from 25%-35%! If you really want to become a "fanatic refunder" you could save up to 50% on your groceries, or even more!

Some people say they never have the time for refunding. Although it is true that more women have full-time outside jobs and perhaps less time for shopping activities...it definitely does *not* take as much time as you might think. You can work on your refunding while watching TV, even while you are talking on the telephone! It can actually become a "fun" hobby that you enjoy while you are cashing in big!

If you would like to take advantage of this moneymaking hobby but don't know how to go about it or where to find the forms, you'll find all the answers and tricks of the trade in easy-to-understand...step-by-step instructions. *CASH IN BIG TODAY!*

How To CASH IN BIG WITH REFUNDS & COUPONS

by Diane Playle

$5.00 ORDER TODAY

MAIL YOUR ORDER WITH PAYMENT TO:

National Paperback Books, Inc

I WANT TO SAVE MONEY ON GROCERIES! PLEASE SEND ME "HOW TO CASH IN BIG ON REFUNDS & COUPONS". I'M ENCLOSING $5.00 + $1.00 SHIPPING.   #904

NAME
       (please print)

ADDRESS

CITY   STATE   ZIP

Tennessee residents add 7% sales tax

Advertisement

GET ALL THE DATES YOU WANT!

NEVER SPEND ANOTHER NIGHT ALONE!

EVERY DAY **SCORES** OF POSSIBILITIES GO RIGHT **BY** YOU—WHEN JUST **SAYING** AND **DOING** THE RIGHT THING COULD PUT **YOU** WITH **MR. RIGHT!**

How To DATE MEN ...and KEEP Them!
by Carol Anne Garret

Have you ever noticed how **some** women seem to get **all** the dates, while others **never** do? Or, have you ever seen an **ugly** girl arm and arm with some gorgeous hunk? Ever wonder about it? **Sure** you have! Did you know there are **reasons** behind this? **How** these women **do** it is no big mystery. They simply know how to make all the **right moves.**

NEVER BE LONELY AGAIN!

Sound impossible? It's **not.** There are tried and true techniques for **attracting males**—**proven** methods that will **work for you,** no matter how poorly you've done with men in the past!

Think of it. By knowing just a few basic principles and faithfully applying them to everyday situations, **you can completely change your love life.**

Let me introduce myself. I'm **Carol Anne Garret,** and like thousands of other women, I used to be on the **losing side** of the dating game. Yes, I was one of the walking wounded, alone and desperate. I tried everything

—singles bars, discos, computerized dating services, personal columns. Nothing worked.

Then I discovered the dynamic **secrets of attracting men**—and the strangest part is that those "secrets" were so **obvious** that I wonder now how I ever **missed** them!

I have gathered all of my findings into a provocative new book with a complete list of all the **right** moves and all the **wrong** moves I've discovered women make with men.

•EVERY WOMEN SHOULD HAVE THIS BOOK!

You don't have to spend another minute wondering when that special man will come into your life! He may be closer than you think—at your job, in a restaurant, or maybe living right next door to you.

Whoever he is, if you want to pursue him romantically, you have to **meet him** first. And to do that you must first **get his attention.** How will you attract him? Will he like you enough to ask you out?

How will you know if your timing is right, or what to say? How will you know if he is serious? Will he stand you up?

LEARN THE SIMPLE SECRETS...

MY BOOK ANSWERS ALL THESE QUESTIONS AND MORE! HERE'S JUST A SAMPLE OF IT'S CONTENTS:

• **TECHNIQUES THAT MAKE MEN SEXUALLY INSECURE** (AND WHAT'S **MORE** SURPRISING, THEY **LOVE** IT!)

• **5 METHODS OF GETTING DATES—WITHOUT RISKING REJECTION!**

• **25 RULES FOR MEETING MEN—PLUS 25 RULES FOR KEEPING THEM!**

• **WHAT MEN LOOK FOR IN WOMEN**—100 COMMENTS FROM SINGLE MEN (YOU'LL FIND THAT WHAT THEY THINK AND SAY IS EXTREMELY REVEALING!)

• **HOW TO UNLOCK WITHIN YOURSELF THE SECRETS OF MANIPULATING MEN!** (HAVE THEM FALLING ALL OVER YOU AND CHASING AFTER YOUR EVERY DESIRE!)

• **7 DYNAMIC SECRETS OF ATTRACTING MEN** (AND THEY'LL WORK FOR **YOU,** NO MATTER WHAT YOU LOOK LIKE!)

DON'T DELAY! ORDER TODAY! FULL 30-DAY MONEY BACK GUARANTEE

If you are not **delighted** with the results after trying the proven techniques outlined in "How To Date Men– and Keep Them!"

GARCO SYSTEMS DEPT. G

PLEASE INCLUDE $2.00 PER BOOK FOR POSTAGE & HANDLING

DEAR CAROL ANNE: YES! I WANT TO WIN AT THE DATING GAME! ENCLOSED PLEASE FIND $10.95, PLUS $2 (P&H) FOR "HOW TO DATE MEN - AND KEEP THEM!" TOTAL ENCLOSED_____

NAME _____
ADDRESS _____
CITY _____ STATE _____ ZIP _____

Send Check or Money Order No C.O.D.s

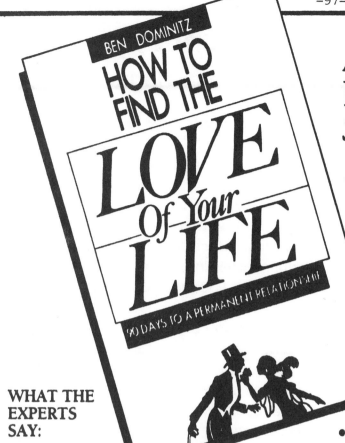

WHAT THE EXPERTS SAY:

On November 11, 1985, a review of How to Find the Love of Your Life appeared in the prestigious **Publishers Weekly** magazine. Here are a few excerpts from that review:

"**How to Find the Love of Your Life** by Ben Dominitz contains much practical advice for those single people in search of a compatible POS (person of opposite sex)... The book rejects both the passivity of chance encounters and the frenetic activity of singles bars...Dominitz gives hints on WHOM to call, HOW to call, WHAT to say, and WHAT to do... The advice is down-to-earth, the tone is never demeaning or patronizing..."

And here's what Dr. Alan Loy McGinnis, leading psychologist and best-selling author of **The Friendship Factor**, says:

"Finally, here is a book that offers genuine help. It's both compelling and highly effective . . . I recommend it enthusiastically to anyone in search of long-lasting love."

So if you or others you know are looking for some straight answers to today's most important question, make sure to order this extraordinary guide today.

Say "Goodbye" to loneliness.
Order your copy today!

At last!
Real Answers for *Sensitive People*

All of us, at one time or another, have experienced the destructive effects of the mating game. Especially for sensitive men and women, it is a loathsome ritual. The fear of rejection; the dating of incompatible people; the awkward, artificial conversations; the why-did-I-go-out-with-him/her feeling afterward — all come with the territory.

You NO LONGER have to put up with this nonsense! In this ground-breaking new book, author Ben Dominitz will show you how to develop an exciting and highly effective campaign that will lead you to the LOVE of YOUR LIFE within the next 90 days.

Among the areas covered:

- Why you should forget about "chance encounters," singles bars, and parties as a way to meet your mate.
- Why the "first date" is among the WORST ways of getting to know someone else and how you can replace it with an incredibly effective alternative.
- How to overcome men's fear of intimacy ("must read" for BOTH men and women).
- Why the best singles are "hidden" and how you can use an old-fashioned idea for meeting an unlimited number in the next 90 days.
- Seven steps to creating greater intimacy in a new relationship.

And much, much more.

HOW TO FIND THE LOVE OF YOUR LIFE IS ALSO A WONDERFUL GIFT TO GIVE TO SOMEONE YOU CARE ABOUT!

- ✂ - -

Dear People:

Please rush me_____ copies of How to Find the Love of Your Life at only **$8.95**   **#1783**

I wish to pay by (check one):
☐ M.O.   ☐ Check

Enclosed is the amount of $ _____plus $2 shipping
(plus $_____sales tax, if applicable), for a total of
$ _____(in U.S. funds only).

Name _____

Address _____

City _____ State _____ Zip _____

Tennessee residents add 7% sales tax

National Paperback Books, Inc

"You don't have to be unhappy,
You can help your own troubled marriage."

. . . Cristy Lane

Over 96% of all Americans think the most important thing to them is having a happy home life. Yet, over 50% of marriages will end in divorce. So many of these can be avoided, when partners can rise above fear, anger and pride. **"How to Help Your Own Troubled Marriage"** will help you overcome these things. Rediscover those wonderful qualities in your spouse, and the closeness that brought you together in the first place.

If you are unhappy, you can make things better. Cristy Lane, beloved gospel singer, and Dr. Laura Ann Stevens, noted marriage counselor, want to help. Together they have written a positive, practical book **"How to Help Your Own Troubled Marriage"** that lets you do just that, even if your partner isn't willing! This book and accompanying cassette tape can assist you, or your children in their marriages.

The authors are well qualified to help you bring love and contentment back to your relationship. Cristy Lane has known and overcome heartbreak. She shares with you her personal experience and methods of self-help in marriage. Dr. Laura Ann Stevens brings to you 10 years of experience and research, to help you overcome marriage problems on your own, without expensive therapists.

This set is also an ideal gift to your children when their marriage is showing signs of trouble they may not yet recognize. You can help them avoid heartbreak and tragedy by sharing with them **"How to Help Your Own Troubled Marriage."** The book and cassette tape will first give the warning signs of problem areas in your marriage, then give specific and realistic steps to correct them: Order **"How to Help Your Own Troubled Marriage"** today. Your marriage may depend on it!

● Privacy of your own home

● Overcome fear, anger and pride

● Learn how to stop fighting dirty

● Your marriage can be saved

Marriage -
Please rush me "How to Help Your Own Troubled Marriage" by Cristy Lane and Dr. Laura Ann Stevens, on your money back guarantee for only $9.95.

1. **How to Help Your Own Troubled Marriage** (book and cassette)	
How to Help Your Own Troubled Marriage	$9.95
Postage and handling	$2.00
Total	

Name _____
Address _____
City _____ State _____ Zip _____

HOW TO GET FREE MEDICAL CARE!

America's Best Kept Secret ...
... Revealed To You — At Last

Did you know that there are over 4,500 hospitals located in all fifty states that are required by Federal Law to provide FREE MEDICAL CARE?!

It's TRUE! But — to take advantage of this amazing bonanza you have to learn two things:

1. Exactly which hospital to go to in your area.
2. Exactly what to say when you get there.

THIS IS THE INFORMATION THAT HAS BEEN HIDDEN FROM YOU LONG ENOUGH!

Now sit down in a comfortable chair and prepare to have your eyes opened!

NEW GUIDEBOOK REVEALS FREE HEALTH CARE SECRET.

If you are afraid and worry about not having enough hospitalization for emergency room service or for any hospital service at all, FEAR NO MORE!

If you are unemployed and have lost your health insurance coverage and need hospitalization — PUT YOUR MIND AT EASE!

Finally — If you need hospital care but can't afford it (for any reason) REST ASSURED!

Biohio Research, a small, privately held think-tank located near a famed Cleveland clinic, has just published an explosive new guidebook exposing the Health Care Discovery of the Century! This amazing guidebook entitled, "HOW TO GET FREE HOSPITAL CARE ANYWHERE IN AMERICA!", contains only 27 pages and can be read and understood in less than 30 minutes. Yet it fully explains this astonishing law in simple language so you can put it to work immediately.

YES — as soon as you finish reading this amazing book you will have the knowledge to get up to $10,000.00 or more worth of FREE MEDICAL CARE anywhere in the USA — no matter what your age is — even if you are now on Medicare or Medicaid!

Think of it! Any Age Qualifies!

SWORN TESTIMONIAL

"HOW TO GET FREE HOSPIAL CARE ANYWHERE IN AMERICA!" has been a real GOD-SEND for us. Thank you, thank you, thank you!
Mrs. Deborah T., Cincinnatti, OH

Here is just a sample of the FREE MEDICAL CARE awaiting you:

- Hospital Emergency room service for accidental injuries
- Surgical procedures of all kinds
- Pregnancy and childbirth
- Nursing home care for the aged
- Mental health and Psychological care
- Treatment for diseases of all kinds etc., etc.

As you can easily see any type of medical care you may ever need you can receive absolutely FREE, once you apply the secret law revealed in "HOW TO GET FREE HOSPITAL CARE ANYWHERE IN AMERICA!"

You can even apply for a reimbursement if you paid for medical service before you knew about this program! YES — UNCLE SAM WILL SEND YOU A BIG, FAT CHECK FOR PAST MEDICAL BILLS!

For a limited time only you will also receive the following Special Bonus.

SPECIAL BONUS

In addition to the guidebook you will also receive — at no extra charge — a complete list of all the hospitals in your entire state where you can get THE FREE MEDICAL CARE described in the guidebook. There are several in your own area — Guaranteed!

Now there is one more thing you must know. It is the most important part of this publicity statement.

THIS IS POWERFUL INFORMATION WHICH HAS BEEN SUPPRESSED FOR 39 YEARS!

The secret law revealed in "HOW TO GET FREE HOSPITAL CARE ANYWHERE IN AMERICA!" has been hidden since the end of WW II — only a very few have benefited. It has remained unpublicized for nearly four decades — a virtual secret! But now, even as you read this message, it's very existance is being threatened by the powers that be.

DON'T BE LEFT OUT!

Take advantage of this rare opportunity while it lasts! Learn how to use this secret law now — before it's too late!

"HOW TO GET FREE HOSPITAL CARE ANYWHERE IN AMERICA!" has been called the greatest HOPE anyone could ever receive. IT CAN SAVE YOU THOUSANDS UPON THOUSANDS OF DOLLARS IN MEDICAL BILLS!

GUARANTEE
Satisfaction Guaranteed

If not satisfied for any reason, return guidebook in undamaged condition within 30 days and receive a full, prompt refund — NO QUESTIONS ASKED!

Because the nature of this guidebook is so controversial, this ad may never be repeated. Send for your copy today, this very minute, while this offer is still in effect. Clip and mail the coupon below with only $10 at once. You risk nothing and save everything — maybe even your own life!

ORDER NOW!

YOUR FREE HOSPITAL CARE COUPON

BIOHIO RESEARCH

¡! YES — Rush me a copy of "HOW TO GET FREE HOSPITAL CARE ANYWHERE IN AMERICA!". I understand that I can receive an immediate no questions asked refund within 30 days of receipt if I am not satisfied for any reason. On that basis, I am enclosing only $10.

PLEASE include $1 cash for special handling and rush shipping.

NAME _____

ADDRESS _____

CITY _____

STATE _____ ZIP_____

YOUR GUIDEBOOK WILL BE SHIPPED THE SAME DAY YOUR ORDER IS RECEIVED
© 1986 Biohio Research

WRITING

COPYRIGHTED IN YOUR **OWN** NAME

BOOKS, BOOKLETS, MANUALS, REPORTS, NEWSLETTERS — "HOW TO" MATERIAL OF EVERY SIZE AND DESCRIPTION for the GIANT MAILORDER BOOKTRADE.

GO WHERE THE ACTION IS — GO FOR THE BIG, BIG BUCKS

MILLIONS of books are sold (by mail) each year by the book-of-the-month clubs, hundreds of small mailorder dealers and individual authors. SELF-HELP books are devoured by Americans and Canadians at an incredible rate. Yet, most writers have overlooked this extremely lucrative market — the easiest of all markets to break. Here's a chance for YOU to capitalize on it.

If your mind is swirling with ideas, this book will show you HOW to turn your ideas into INFORMATIVE manuscripts that will help other people - and can make you money - lots of money.

With my guide book, you can ease yourself gently into a "second-career" and enjoy a very full and prosperous INDEPENDENT writer's life. No editors, no subsidy or no vanity publishers are involved - no one else is going to cut themselves in for a "piece of the action".

It's yours - ALL YOUR OWN - You stay in complete control of your own books, booklets, folios, manuals or other publications. . .every step of the way.

I SHOW YOU HOW

My instructions, illustrations and exercises are such that you can very easily understand exactly what you need to do - and how to do it at your own pace. Nothing is left dangling. The instructions are written just as if you and I were talking alone in my workshop. You will get PRACTICAL INSTRUCTIONS - no fancy theories, no amateur suggestions - strictly VALUABLE PROFESSIONAL POINTERS.

I'll take the risk. You keep the guidebook for 45 full days. Read every word. If not satisfied, return it for you money back. No questions asked.

FULL MONEY-BACK GUARANTEE!

Order from:

National Paperback Books, Inc

**A BIG 8½ x 11 BOOK
176 PAGES, 278 ILLUSTRATIONS**

DISCOVER HOW to start small and pyramid your profits at a fantastic rate.

When you write a book - even a small book - people look at you in awe, with pride, with respect, with envy, with astonishment (that you could even do it) and with an inner desire to do the same thing.

YOU ARE TOLD HOW

- to write about anything
- to prepare your first folio
- to develop your specialty
- to use a $25,000 idea
- to copyright your work
- to find time to write
- to develop more ideas
- to start small
- to pyramid profits
- to price your material
- to create the right titles
- 123 mind-expanding topics
- to place inexpensive advts
- to keep records

That's a mere sampling. The guidebook provides you with full particulars, clearly and concisely explained and illustrated on all important phase of Writing & Selling information. Completely devoid of theory, you profit from tested principles that work on any type of book, folio, or manual you can possibly ever dream about writing. It shows you how to COPYRIGHT and retain complete control of everything you write:
Reap ALL the profits for yourself.

The techniques are equally applicable to simple or to sophisticated works of informative writing - any size, any style.

READ WHAT OTHERS SAY

"I have been waiting for such a long time to start writing, but no one previously helped me constructively. So I just gave up. Now I have something I can do by myself and on my own, thanks to you." **Mrs. G.A.R., York, PA**

"I am retired, looking for a way to go. I found it in your book." **B. Karr, Phoenix, AZ**

"This book reveals absolutely everything, precisely and clearly." **Leo Minton, Editor, Money Making Magic**

"I have enjoyed and profited from your book." **J.J. Stepp, Atlanta, GA**

"This book is the best I've ever read. And I've read them all on this subject." **Steve Williams, Book Reviewer**

I want you to know that you're not dealing with a pipedreamer, but with a success-oriented seasoned pro. My published work has appeared in every state of the USA and in 39 foreign lands. I live very comfortably on a secluded mountainside where tranquility is supreme.

You too could live, love and play anywhere - anywhere you chose. Are you worth $15 to give yourself a try?

Then for goodness sake DO IT!

Jay Barnes
Author & Publisher

················ MAIL TODAY ································

YES! I Love to Write. Show me how to crack this giant market.
Please **RUSH** my copy of "HOW TO MAKE MONEY WRITING & SELLING SIMPLE IMFORMATION.**   Here's my $15 at no risk.   #317
Tennessee residents add 7% sales tax./Add $1 per book for shipping & handling

PLEASE PRINT OR TYPE

Name _____
Address _____
City _____ State _____ Zip _____

HOW TO ...

GO TO COLLEGE FREE
ATTEND ACCREDITED, RESPECTED COLLEGES AND UNIVERSITIES
ABSOLUTELY FREE
(EVEN RECEIVE MONEY FOR GOING TO SOME!)

WHO NEEDS A COLLEGE EDUCATION?

- You!
- Your children!
- Your grandchildren!
- Everyone needs a college education. It's the American Way ... the way to financial independence and self-esteem.

WHO CAN QUALIFY FOR A FREE OR LOW COST COLLEGE EDUCATION?

- Not everyone, of course
- But far more people than you might think!
- Probably even you can qualify!

College aid is available! Many people fail to realize just how much aid is really there, just for the asking. And many others believe that they could not possibly qualify for college aid. But did you know that

OVER $100 BILLION

is available each year to families who can establish the need for financial aid?

Second only to a home, just one child's college education is typically a family's single biggest investment. Will your child have the opportunity to attend college? Will you do all in your power to give him or her that important headstart in life?

BUT I'M NOT POOR, HOW CAN I QUALIFY?

Much easier than you might think! And the dynamic book "How To Obtain Maximum College Financial Aid" will show you how affluent and destitute families alike can qualify for free and low cost college aid.

Typically, 63% of the affluent who know how to apply receive college financial aid. And this doesn't even consider the huge numbers of less affluent people who receive college financial aid each year! Read case histories, the rules, the strategies explained in this comprehensive book and you, too, will know how to apply and qualify for college aid.

Whether you are in a low or high income bracket, you may qualify for college assistance for you or your family. But how will you ever know without reading this dynamic book. Isn't a college education and the opportunity of a lifetime worth $10.00?

OVER $5 BILLION IN LOW INTEREST FUNDS

That's just the amount of federally subsidized loans that go unused each year! Many people simply don't know that these funds are available. That's why you need "How To Obtain Maximum College Financial Aid" now ... to assist you in discovering how and where to apply for maximum aid.

Here's just a partial list of the contents of this dynamic book. Read them all, as you're bound to find at least several that apply to your situation.

Cost of college education ... today and tomorrow

How eligibility for college financial aid is determined

How to fill in the forms

How to negotiate with a financial aid officer

The selection process

What may disqualify you from receiving aid

How to legitimately reduce your income and assets in order to qualify for financial aid

How to avoid consideration of certain income assets (for the more affluent)

Federal government aid programs

Private and institutional aid programs

Special programs

Hot to best use real estate, IRA's, SEP's, annuities and life insurance to your advantage in financing a college education

Detailed information about the six most widely used government programs

Information on lesser known government programs

The financial aid package

College work study programs

Guaranteed student loans (GSL)

Health education programs

Sample situations

Military academy scholarships

Directory for finding guaranteed student loans

Directory for obtaining information about state aid

And much, much more!

Fellowships, minority, bilingual military and medical grants and scholarships

It doesn't matter whether your college choice is Yale, Harvard, your state university, an out-of-state university, or even your local junior college. Financial aid is available. You must only know how to apply and qualify!

There will always be some families who are not able to qualify for financial aid. For those who believe they may not qualify for one reason or another, and for those families whose children must or wish to work during college, we provide an additional thoroughly researched book that provides detailed information about where and how to get good-paying, career-oriented college jobs.

Each year, informed students earn well over $5,000 for part-time or cooperative education work. Just think how this would help with your college expenses ... even when you do receive financial aid!

Over 1,000 colleges and universities participate in cooperative education work plans that match your course of study or degree plan. You learn while you earn! Often the very same employer will offer you, upon graduation, permanent employment at well above the normal starting salary and entry level.

Just think what a headstart you will have on your fellow graduates upon graduation. Think how your actual career-related job experience will look on your resume!

Since the Federal government is the single largest employer, a portion of this detailed book explains how and where the student can find the schools that participate in cooperative education with the government. Explained are the type of jobs available, which department of the government and the degree levels appropriate to the jobs.

A comprehensive directory of contacts for the different governmental departments is included as a source for obtaining more specific information.

Next, the schools that participate in cooperative education programs are listed with their addresses. Each school is indexed by a wide variety of information such as number of students accepted in the program, degree plans involved, whether academic credit is awarded for participation, and many other plan details.

Finally, the "Junior Fellowship Program" for very bright high school seniors is described and program entrance details are explained.

SATISFACTION GUARANTEED

Both books are guaranteed to assist you in obtaining college financial aid or in obtaining a good-paying, career-oriented college job. If you are not satisfied for any reason, simply return your purchase within thirty days for a full refund. You must be satisfied or your money back.

YES! Rush me the following books:

[ ] "How To Obtain Maximum College Financial Aid". Item #1781 .... $10

[ ] How & Where To Get Good-Paying, Career-Oriented College Jobs". Item #1782 .... $10

[ ] Order both books and save $3! $17

[ ] Check; [ ] Money Order;

Add $1 per book for postage and handling

Name _____

Address _____

City _____

State _____ Zip Code _____

Mail Your Order Today To:
    National Paperback Books, Inc

Satisfaction Guaranteed Or Your Money Back
Tennessee residents add 7% sales tax

Is Your Marriage On The Rocks?

AT LAST A FORMULA FOR SAVING YOUR TROUBLED MARRIAGE.... .... AND GETTING RICH IN RETURN

Is your marriage free of troubles?

Can you eliminate all the present problems from the rough relationship with your spouse?

And have none in the future?

Even if you are only living together!

The answer is: *Yes! You Can!*

Not only that......

Working all alone, you can save your marriage from falling apart. By "all alone", I mean, even if you *do not* have the cooperation of your spouse.

Now, I know that sounds incredible. Even a bit ridiculous. Specially, when you look around and find one in every two marriages in trouble.

But, I am not kidding when I say you *can* save your troubled marriage. I mean it! I am proud to present to you a unique way that can solve the problems in your marriage. A way that can eliminate the possibility of separation and divorce.

This is a method by which you can reunite with your partner — physically, mentally and emotionally. *You may even discover for the first time in your life what true love really feels like!*

The plan works whatever the issues in your marriage

I do realize all this is not that simple. Yet, all I ask you is to start working on a set of simplified steps given in my PLAN. Just by doing that, you can *completely* and *permanently* change the quality of your marriage relationship.

My plan will become *your plan* regardless of the issues involved in your marriage. Is it bad health? Not enough money? Unsatisfactory sex life? Difficulty in handling children? Unable to get along with your spouse? All of these? ... And many more?

No problem! This marvelous PLAN is good even if you have almost *given up* on your marriage.

A scientific method based on common sense

When I say I will show you *how* you can save your marriage, *I am not talking about religion.* I don't want to preach you a sermon on the sins of separation and the devil of divorce. I don't want to scare you into accepting an unacceptable way of life.

I only want to tell you that you *are* capable of overriding your domestic complications — *whatever their nature.* I am promising you a unique, scientific method that will appeal to your common sense.

What divorce can do

As we all know, the break-up of marriage is not that easy. Going through the divorce is rarely pleasant. It is full of headaches and heartaches. It is a big drain on person's emotions — and on the purse.

As a result of divorce, many businesses break and many homes have to be sold. Some people lose financial stability; others join poverty line. Divorce is particularly hard on children.

You would enjoy every moment of your life together

Yet, it is really possible to avoid all this . . . with the help of this PLAN.

THE PLAN is guaranteed to help you solve all of the problems in your marriage. It provides emotional support. It gives financial help. It shows variety of ways to reduce your weight and re-develop the strong, vigorous health.

THE PLAN also reveals many novel ways to enjoy the limitless pleasures of sex within the marriage.

It tells you how to deal with your spouse, how to raise trouble-free children, even how to put extra time in your life if you happen to be a busy person.

But the best of all, it shows you how to relax your body and soothe your nerves in order for you to experience that tranquility and peace *within.* Happiness is only another name for this state of mind.

What makes THE PLAN so effective is the numerous analysis charts, illustrations, check-lists and selected, *ready-to-use* ideas . . . the practical, down-to-earth *specific* ideas that a common man and woman can easily use and benefit from.

In short . . . .

You can actually enjoy *every moment* of your life together — with a renewed sense of self-confidence and self-worth. *(You may even become financially rich!* More on this later.)

If you do have the desire, I have the way

Let me say this once again. If you *do have the desire,* I have *the way.* If you *do want to* save your marriage, I will show you *how.*

I will reveal to you the secrets and details of my simple, fool-proof plan. You *yourself* will see the amazing results as you work on it *step by step.*

Don't ignore any steps. Follow THE PLAN to *the letter.*

If you do that seriously, you simply cannot fail. There is a built-in success in this method. This is due to the fact that THE PLAN is the fine blending of old-world wisdom and the modern research into the subject.

The whole program has been appropriately named: "How To Save Your Troubled Marriage — even if your spouse doesn't cooperate".

That's right . . . . even if your spouse doesn't cooperate!

The beauty of this method is that you can start working on this PLAN all alone, despite non-cooperation — *even opposition* — of your spouse. In fact, you should not even mention it to your partner until your own steps are well underway. Your partner can later join in at any time he or she is ready.

Working all by yourself, you will be able to transform the resentment, fear, suspicion and hate in your relationship into harmony, peace, loyalty and love.

What about the presently stable marriages?

Even *the presently stable marriages* can utilize the method in order to avoid any problems arising in the future. This simple PLAN is designed to continuously increase the closeness and love between husband and wife.

Because . . . . it would immensely help *strengthen* and *deepen* their mutual relationship.

And, the couples that are simply living together?

Since, the couples living together often face the same set of human relationship problems as their married counterparts, they too can profit from the many-sided values of this versatile PLAN.

Cheaper than a single visit to a marriage counselor

This powerful PLAN is regularly priced at a nominal amount of $25. However, for a limited time, I am offering it at a reduced price of $12.95.

Is the new-found love and the renewed happiness in your life worth this token amount? Is the sparkle in the eyes of your innocent children worth it? What about the quiet confidence in your heart that your home can never *ever* break again? Is that worth this token price?

Incidentally, the price is less than the cost of a single visit to psycho-therapist or to a marriage counselor.

Never before has this burning issue been so completely analyzed and simplfied into a definite, no-nonsense, step-by-step solution.

Satisfaction guaranteed or your money refunded in full

I am so confident of the positive results THE PLAN can bring in your life that I offer to refund your complete purchase price within an extended period of six weeks — if you are not *fully* satisfied with it *for whatever reasons.*

During these six weeks, any time you ask for it, your purchase price will be promptly refunded. Just return THE PLAN in good salable condition. *There will be no questions asked.*

I will send you one more thing — FREE. This is a Special Report: "Five Steps To The Financial Freedom". Five common sense steps to acquiring wealth easily and enjoying it fully. *Your personal net-worth will keep on rising dramatically.*

The approach is so obvious that most people easily lose sight of it. Many successful persons are known to use only portions of it. But, *any working man or woman* can use the method *in its entirety* with unbelievable results.

This getting rich report is yours to keep FREE, even if you decide to return the main PLAN.

Because of the introductory nature of this offer, only a limited number of PLANS are available at the moment. Quantities are, therefore, restricted to just two PLANS per family (one for you and one for your spouse).

Also, delivery can be guaranteed only to those who respond within 45 days of this printed notice. After that, orders wil be taken on a "first come first served" basis as long as the supplies last.

To order, just write your name and address on the coupon and send it with $12.95 to Shree Sidhwani, 7 Maize Court, Melville, N.Y. 11747.

Remember, this exclusive all-in-one PLAN is *NOT* available anywhere else - *at any price.* The only way to guarantee prompt delivery is to send your order right now.

©Shree Sidhwani - 1988, 7 Maize Court, Melville, N.Y. 11747

Highlights of THE PLAN:

- Not a religious sermon. A simple, workable, logical method designed to focus primarily on your own individual marriage.
- Works despite non-cooperation — even opposition — of your spouse.
- Eliminates the chances of presently stable marriages from going sour in the future.
- Equally effective even for couples simply living together.

CAN YOU USE ANY OF THESE?

THE PLAN does not help your marriage alone. Just look at some of the additional benefits you receive — simultaneously — as you work on it step by step:

- You can utilize the basic principles and ideas of THE PLAN for *making more and more money faster than ever before.* This strategy is briefly outlined in the FREE bonus report "Five Steps To The Financial Freedom".
- You can once again *regain your lost health.* You will know how to *combat fatigue* and never, ever, get easily tired.
- With the easy natural ideas in THE PLAN, you won't have to fight with your food anymore. Yet, you could enjoy *permanent weight control* and maintain *the perfect body shape.*
- You can learn *valuable sexual skills* that can turn every one of your *sexual encounters into a truly pleasurable experience.* This could earn you an unfailing devotion of your partner.
- You will know exactly how to *train your children* to turn them into well-behaved, obedient, happy and successful individuals.
- Certain simple ideas in THE PLAN can *make you a well-liked, sought-after person* in your society and in your circle of friends.

Shree Sidhwani

Okay Shree. I guess I have nothing to lose. Rush me THE PLAN "How To Save Your Troubled Marriage". Enclosed is my check or money order.

If, however, I return your material — for any reason — within six weeks of ordering, refund my full purchase price promptly.

In any case, your special report on Financial Freedom wil be mine to keep FREE just for trying THE PLAN. On that basis, here is my $12.95.

(N.Y. State residents add appropriate sales tax)

Name _____
(Please Print Clearly)

Address _____

City _____

State _____ Zip _____

SORRY — NO COD's
(All foreign orders please add three dollars)

$100,000 PUBLISHING YOUR OWN MANUALS, BOOKS, OR BOOKLETS...

START WITH PENNIES...

...Yes, that's right. With today's modern printing methods you can publish just a few copies to get started. Then, as your sales build up you can order more copies.

MORE BUCKS FROM BOOKS...

...Why sell the books that others publish, when you can start your own publishing business in a spare bedroom, basement or garage. This very day thousands of new publishers have found their own goldmine by publishing books that they prepared in their spare time. No fancy offices are needed. Do all your selling by mail.

NEW SMALL PUBLISHER'S SUCCESS...

...14,000 new small publishers have developed in just the past few years. Each of them have their own specialty. Everything from books on sailing to making your car engine get 200 miles per gallon. Everyone needs information and facts just to survive today.

TELL WHAT YOU KNOW...

You are an expert at something. Maybe its Household Hints that you have accumulated. One woman sold over a million copies of a book of this type. Or possibly your information is in a specialized field. Others need to know what you know and they will pay to get your information.

HOW MUCH PROFIT...

...Would you believe it if I told you that books costing 10¢ each are today selling for $10 retail. I can state this as a fact since I personally publish two that fit that profit range myself. That is 1000% PROFIT. Why don't I put this in the headline? Because to those who do not know the publishing business it would be unbelievable, even though it is true.

WHAT TO WRITE...

...Let me give you ideas of what's selling these days. You'll find it in my fat manual, HOW TO PUBLISH YOUR OWN BOOK SUCCESSFULLY. Suppose you can't write! Don't let that stop you. If you'll just get your material together there are plenty of people you can hire for a few bucks to fix it up proper for selling. I tell you all about it in my manual.

MAIL ORDER SELLING...

...Publish and sell all by mail. Sell retail. Sell wholesale in big lots. I will tell you all the methods and the best way to go about each one. It's simple when you know how, but you sure could lose your shirt if you don't have all the inside facts and information.

$100,000

SECRETS UNLIMITED...

...One man printed his first book very cheaply with just 100 copies. This was a manual on how to win prize contests. Now he has sold over 100,000. What you need to be a success in low cost publishing is the inside secrets. Successful publishers know how but they don't give out the facts. Let me open the secrets of "Cheepie" publishing success to you. I can't write all the books that are needed today so I want to share my publishing success secrets with you. Will you let me help you get started?

LET ME HELP YOU...

...Yes, I could sit down with you and show you step-by-step how to publish your book and make it a best seller but I would have to charge you a bundle for this. Instead, I put everything in my manual, HOW TO PUBLISH YOUR OWN BOOK SUCCESSFULLY and it sells for only $10 a copy. This is certainly a lot less than the $1,000 I would have to charge for personal consultation. It's all there for you to read and follow the simple instructions.

SELL TO LIBRARIES AND BOOK STORES...

...There is a whole big cash market waiting for you in libraries and book stores. More books... more sales... more bucks. How do I know? I have done it and want you to see for yourself.

PRINTING IS NOT PUBLISHING...

...A word to the wise. Some people do not know that printing a book is only one small part of publishing. Selling the book is the ALL IMPORTANT part. There are thousands of printers waiting to do printing for you... but you must be careful and select the right one or it could cost you many dollars in sales. A real publisher knows how to sell his books. That's what I want to show you!

MAKE MONEY WITH BOOKLETS, REPORTS, DIRECTORIES...

...A book by any other name is still your opportunity for publishing success. Many $3 booklets cost only 5¢ to print. Are they worth $3? Certainly. I once paid $25 for a manual. As a result of that investment I have been marketing a book for over ten years that has sold over 75,000 copies. You can do the same.

FREE REPORT WITH YOUR MANUAL...

I have prepared a special report "How To Get Your Books Printed Cheap" and I will send a copy with your manual if you order within 30 days.

GET STARTED TODAY...

...No one but yourself is holding you back from publishing success. You have it within your own power to send this very day for your success publishing secrets. I have put it together for you. All you have to do is ask for it.

30 DAY MONEY BACK GUARANTEE...

...All I want you to do is get HOW TO PUBLISH YOUR OWN BOOK SUCCESSFULLY in your own hands. Once you see it and feel it in front of you I know that you will wonder why you ever hesitated for a moment. Look at it. If it isn't all that I have said it is... just shoot it back for a refund.

RELEASE YOUR GOLD MINE...

...You already have what it takes to be a success in publishing. Let me release to you the secrets that can make it all come true for you. I have published over 15 books. Many have been selling for ten years or more. The coupon below provides the way for you to be a SUCCESS PUBLISHER, too!

3rd MAJOR PRINTING
THOUSANDS SOLD AT $15...
NOW GET THIS SOFTBOUND
EDITION FOR ONLY $10.

_____ Yes, I want to get rich publishing books and start small. Here is my $10. send "HOW TO PUBLISH YOUR OWN BOOK SUCCESSFULLY and a copy of the FREE report, "How to Get your Books Printed Cheap". #1723

Name _____

Address _____

City, State, Zip _____

Order from: National Paperback Books, Inc

Add $1 per book for shipping & handling

Tennessee residents add 7% sales tax

It's easy, fun and very profitable....

SELL BOOKS BY MAIL

...these two great manuals
tell you where the money is and how to get it!

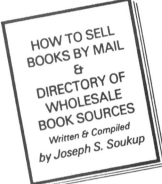

HOW TO SELL BOOKS BY MAIL & DIRECTORY OF WHOLESALE BOOK SOURCES

Written & Compiled
by Joseph S. Soukup

BOOK DEALERS DROPSHIP DIRECTORY

Written & Compiled
by Al Galasso

This combination instruction manual and valuable source guide can help you establish a profitable mail order book business. Mr. Soukup is a highly respected "old pro" at selling books by mail. He teaches from experience, not from a textbook.

This manual is easy to read and easy to use. Discover how to:

► *Get started on a shoestring*
► *Get the most from your advertising and printing dollar*
► *Secrets of result-getting classified ads*
► *How to sell direct from the ad*
► *Effective direct mail selling*
► *Build your own mailing lists*
► *How to test for best results*
► *The "best time" for mail order selling*
► *Rapidly build your mail order book business*

In addition to the above advice, you will also have an extensive directory of wholesale book sources at your fingertips. From Astrology to Zoology, from Business books to Joke books, the information and addresses are all here! *Buy low—sell high! Make up to 400% profits and more!*

How to Sell Books by Mail & Directory of Wholesale Book Sources will help you make money, part time or full time in the fascinating mail order book, manual and information business. *A bargain at only $10.*

DROPSHIPPING is a unique marketing method that enables you to sell books, collect cash in advance, then have the books shipped direct to your customers from the prime publisher. You keep 50% of the monies for easy work. No need to stock any expensive inventory. As a mail order bookseller, you'll have access to some of the hottest-selling books available today in a wide variety of popular categories including: **business, self-help, metaphysical, health, how-to, crafts, finance and more!** As an independent publisher, you'll be able to offer more books to your own list of satisfied customers. This expanded third edition of the BOOK DEALERS DROPSHIP DIRECTORY describes dropshipping in detail and reveals how both publishers and mail order booksellers can use it successfully. After all, some of the largest companies in America use dropshipping services every day. Now you can, too!

The names and addresses of hundreds of reliable dropship publishers and distributors are featured, plus a listing of one or more titles that they carry. Many of these sources also offer big wholesale discounts if you ever choose to stock books and fill your own orders. However, *dropshipping will get you started in the fascinating and lucrative book business for peanuts.*

Now you can start a great home business with little capital and build it into a fabulous moneymaker. *This information-packed directory is worth many times our low price of only $7.*

━━━━━━━━━━━━━━ ORDER FORM ━━━━━━━━━━━━━━

For fast delivery, mail your order to: National Paperback Books, Inc

SAVE!
Save $3 Order Both Great Manuals for Only $14

Tennessee residents add 7% sales tax
☐ Enclosed is $10 plus $1 postage/handling. Send *HOW TO SELL BOOKS BY MAIL.*
☐ Enclosed is $7 plus $1 postage/handling. Send *BOOK DEALERS DROPSHIP DIRECTORY.*
☐ Enclosed is $14 plus only $1 postage/handling. I want both manuals.

I am paying by: ☐ Check   ☐ Money Order
Name _____ Address _____
City _____ State _____ Zip _____

ORDER WITHOUT RISK—SATISFACTION GUARANTEED—30-DAY MONEY-BACK GUARANTEE

HOW TO START AND OPERATE YOUR OWN PROFITABLE BUSINESS AT HOME

Join the hundreds of successful beginners who are prospering in their own profitable businesses at home!

Are you getting tired of your *nine to five* job just to make ends meet? Have you tried to start your own *business* at home and failed?

Now, at last, for those who seriously want to start their own profitable business at home there is a *guaranteed* way. It's called *"How to Start and Operate Your Own Profitable Business at Home"*. This incredible book is complete. It covers everything from "A" to "Z". It's *easy* to read and explains everything you need to know — *step-by-step* — to start your own successful business at home.

The Possible Dream

For many people, starting their own money-making business seems like a dream that never comes true. They think it requires special talent and lots of capital and only a few can succeed. But nothing is further from reality than this thought. Just look around you. You see lots of *self-made millionaires* with no formal education who started with nothing. One thing they all had in common, however, is a strong *belief*. They believed in THEMSELVES and in their *IDEAS*. I know you *believe* in yourself, too. Now you, too, can start any one of these seven *most* profitable businesses revealed in this incredible book. Hundreds of people have made thousands of dollars through each one of these businesses.

Seven Most Profitable Businesses

These are the most profitable home based businesses that can be found in America today. The amazing thing about every one of these ventures is that it does not require much capital. Unlike the majority of businesses where you need a large capital outlay of $10,000 to $15,000 just to get started, you can start on a *shoe string* and make a great deal of money in a short period of time. Another unique feature is that you can work at home. You don't need an office, you can start at your kitchen table. And you'll probably make so much money that you can quit your job if you want to.

Proof

None of these enterprises are get-rich-quick schemes. They are, however, proven get-rich-slow programs. If you ever dreamed of the freedom of operating your own profitable business, then this is for you! While you are reading this, hundreds of people are making thousands of dollars every month — part time — with these *fascinating* ventures. Now you have the opportunity to do exactly what they are doing. You too can easily be the proud owner of your own successful business, earning thousands of dollars in your spare time — and best of all — in the privacy of your own home!

Start Now

This amazing book gives you step-by-step instruction on how to start your own favorite business at home and prosper in the years to come. There are seven hot, profitable programs you can choose from. Pick the one which interests you the most. Every one of them is *proven* to make you money. They've made thousands of dollars for their owners. And now, for the first time ever, they are all revealed in this fascinating book. So place your order NOW... Don't wait to get in on this incredible opportunity! Simply fill in the handy order form, enclose *cash, check* or *money order*, and mail it to us TODAY!

Contents

BUSINESS NO. 1
How to Start and Operate Your Own Profitable Mail Order Business at Home

BUSINESS NO. 2
How to Make a Fortune with Classified Ads

BUSINESS NO. 3
How to Set Up Your Own In-House Advertising Agency...and Save Up to 17% of Advertising Costs

BUSINESS NO. 4
How to Sell Information by Mail

BUSINESS NO. 5
How to Publish Your Own Newsletter

BUSINESS NO. 6
How to Start and Operate Your Own Profitable Import/Export Business at Home

BUSINESS NO. 7
How to Make Up to $750 Next Weekend

Free Bonuses

Your book also includes the following three valuable and informative bonuses FREE.

BONUS NO. 1
How to Accomplish Anything You Want in Life

BONUS NO. 2
How to Get Free Publicity for Your Business

BONUS No. 3
Secrets of the Richest People

But, remember — you must order *within 30 days* to receive this fabulous set of FREE bonuses.

Guaranteed

This incredible book is full of valuable information that insiders have kept to themselves for many years. Their secrets have been revealed in this amazing book. We want you to see it for yourself. Send in your order now. Read it. Study it for 10 days. If you don't agree that it's worth at least 100 times what you have paid for, return it within 10 days for a full refund, no questions asked. That is our IRON-CLAD GUARANTEE.

© 1986, 1982 JOHN WRIGHT

ORDER FORM

Please rush my copy of *"How to Start and Operate Your Own Profitable Business at Home"*. I've enclosed $15.00+$2.00 Shipping & Handling.

☐ Cash ☐ Check ☐ Money Order

NAME _____
(Please Print)

ADDRESS_____

CITY _____

STATE _____ ZIP_____

Please send your order to:

Bishop, Barrett & Meyers Publishers,

CA residents add 6% sales tax

HOW TO STOP Smoking

I Invented A Sure-Fire-Way To Stop Smoking! No Withdrawal Pains! It's Virtually Impossible To Gain Weight! No Nervousness! No Bad Temper! No Drugs! No Hypnosis!

Have you ever tried to quit cold turkey? I did, and it was a horrible experience. I couldn't stop thinking about cigarettes. I was almost crazy with withdrawal symptoms, and the compulsive eating wouldn't stop.

I was a cigarette junkie! And I had to face it.

I had tried everything on the market from unpleasant tasting gum you chew to change your taste buds, to cabbage cigarettes. "That's right fellow smokers, you didn't misread that last statement. I said cigarettes made from cabbage. They're awful. Take my word for it."

For years I had tried to stop smoking and was getting nowhere. I was completely frustrated with myself and my lack of any "will-power."

I knew what my problem was, but I couldn't do anything about it. My problem was that every time I tried to stop smoking I found myself making dozens of excuses why I shouldn't stop.

Excuses like: "Who wants to quit anyway. What are you going to do when someone gets you upset and angry over something really stupid. You're just going to start back up again, like you did in the past, so why quit in the first place."

On and on they went ..... one lame excuse after another.

The one I like the best is: "What are you going to do when you go out to a night club or restaurant, with the guys, and everyone is sitting around smoking and you're not?"

Thoughts like these plagued me constantly. To the point where I just plain stopped trying.

I Had To Stop!

I had to stop and I had to do it soon. I was becoming a danger to myself and a menace to everybody around me. Besides that, I had just burned a hole in the drivers seat of my brand new car, and every one of my expensive suits had little burn holes in the front of the pants, that were becoming very embarrassing.

I Hit on Something Different!

I conducted several tests on myself and my friend Kathy. Kathy had been a smoker from age 14 to her present age 30. Over fifteen years of smoking without a break.

The goal we both were trying to reach was simple. **—We both wanted to stop smoking without knowing we were stopping.—** This was tricky, and we both knew very difficult to accomplish. But, at that point in our lives we both knew one thing, if we didn't know anything else. "We definitely did not want to go through withdrawal pains, nor did we want to become overweight by trying to satisfy our need for cigarettes by overeating."

We had tried several different methods over the years all with the same results; We always started smoking again.

Here's The Secret!

We invented a new way to "Stop Smoking" one that would slowly take our craving for cigarettes and completely dismantle it one hour at a time from our habit.

Here's How It Works!

How did your habit begin? How did the habit grow to one pack, two packs, three packs or more a day? Here's the answer. The habit was allowed to schedule itself. It was left unchecked! THE HABIT learned day after day to smoke at frequently repeated times in your day. After all, that's what habit is: something habitual. Our daily routines

are habitual, too. The smoking habit plugs itself into our routines. Many of the little daily stops in our routines become signals to the smoking habit. A little bell seems to go off. Accustomed routines touch off the urge to reach for that smoke.

Well, you can beat the smoking habit at its own game—once you dismantle the body's smoking schedule "one brick at a time." I'm not talking about anything like cold-turkey, either. That hardly ever works for one simple reason: you can't take the whole wall down all at once. The body's schedule of habit is much too strong for that.

Here's What I Discovered!

I discovered a way to change your habit. A Way so simple, that I wonder why no one has ever thought of it before.

My new Stop Smoking Program will show you how to stop smoking without withdrawal pains.
No Cold Turkey!
No Drugs!
No Bad Temper!
No Overeating!
No Gaining Weight!
No Hypnosis!

My New Method will show you how to stop smoking completely. The need and desire to smoke will be gone forever when you use this new method. And the best part is — you won't compensate by chewing gum or eating candy all day.

The Hazards of Smoking!

You know the hazards of smoking, and you know how it sometimes can make your life very uncomfortable. But, if that does not appeal to your sense of well being then lets try greed.

Stop Smoking And Save up to $1,000 A Year!

I know $1,000 dollars a year doesn't sound like much, but in ten years that's $10,000 dollars. Look back ten years ago. If you had stoped smoking and started putting away the money you spent on cigarettes, in a interest bearing account, today with current interest rates you would have $27,000.00 in the bank. Just think what you could do with Twenty-Seven Thousand Dollars right now.

All that aside. Let me show you how to beat the cigarette habit. I promise you won't even know you're stopping. **But, please don't wait.**

Don't Let This Opportunity Slip By You! To let this opportunity slip by you would be a shame. If you put this page down without ordering, the opportunity may not be available to you again. You may never know how great it feels not being tied to cigarettes everyday.

Order Today! Order your complete program titled: "How To Stop Smoking!" right Now! **I promise you will be thrilled** with your new life style and I guarantee that this **"first-time-offered".....** Stop Smoking Program, is different from anything you have ever seen before, it's very effective and very easy to use. **Take my word for it, it is really easy to use.**

100% Money-Back Guarantee

"What if I don't like it?" You Can Return it!

I'll Give You A 90 Day Money-Back Guarantee. If at any time after receiving the "Stop Smoking!" program you want to return it, for any reason, do so. I will immediately refund your $5.95 along with my appreciation and highest regards for you, for at least having given it a try.
There will be No questions asked! No hassles! No delays! Just a cheerful and prompt refund.

Take the time "Right Now". Pick up your pen. Fill out the "Express Order Form" below, and mail it in Today! In a few days time you will have my "Stop Smoking!" program in your hands. Use the information provided and quit cigarettes forever.

Don't put it off. Send the "Order Form" in today. I will give your order immediate attention the moment it arrives. And your "Stop Smoking" program will go into the mail that very afternoon.

Offer Carries A Full 90 Day Money-Back Guarantee.

My Office phone number is

© *John Van Patten 1987*

My Stop Smoking Program is being Published and Marketed by New Start Publications, Inc. —a substantial long standing Corporation— additional reassurance that your Money Back Guarantee is well protected.
Order More Than One!
They Make Great Secret Gifts For Your Friends.

— — — — — Express Order Form — — — — —

New Start Publications, Inc.
John Van Patten

Dear John, please RUSH me my Stop Smoking program titled: **"How To Stop Smoking!"** only with the understanding that I have a full 90 days to test your sure-fire method. If I am not completely satisfied, for any reason, I may simply return "How To Stop Smoking", and you will immediately refund the full purchase price to me. On that basis here is $5.95.

Name _____

Address _____

City _____

State _____ Zip _____
Make Check Payable To: New Start Publications, Inc.

TURN YOUR NEWSPAPERS INTO $$$$ CASH $$$$

Attention ... wage earners, housewives, underpaid workers ... and anyone else who needs an easy, profitable home-run business

What would you say if someone told you that each day ... every day ... you were throwing cash dollars into the garbage? You'd die laughing, right?

FLASH ... You are! Each day that your old, now read newspaper goes into the trash, you're throwing away a gold mine in profits. The cynics who insist that "yesterday's newspaper is today's fishwrap", obviously aren't thinking very far ahead.

VAST MARKET POTENTIAL
Did you know that there are over 15,000 trade, technical and special interest magazines in the nation right now? With more entering the market each week? Most of these publications are relatively small and must pay for their news items. And that's where you—and your yesterday's newspaper come in!

NEWS ITEMS DESPERATELY NEEDED
Newspaper articles that appear in your local newspaper are desperately needed by these magazines. They pay cold, hard cash for local news items of interest to their readers which they would never have seen if people just like yourself did not send them in for publication. A few of the biggies have a full complement of reporters and a large staff to comb the nation for their articles. And a few more subscribe to the national wire services like AP, UPI and K-R. But the vast majority of these magazines have to scratch ... and scratch hard ... for their newsy items.

YOU HOLD THE KEY
You see the material they want every day. They can't afford to subscribe to every newspaper in the nation—or even to a few. And they certainly can't afford the time to scan all those newspapers. *They want to pay you for that information.* They want to pay you $2...$5...$25...$50...even more for the articles that you find, clip and send to them for publication.

DISCOVER HOW
You can discover exactly how to cash in on this vast (and virtually untapped) market by obtaining a copy of *How To Turn Your Newspapers Into $$$$ Cash $$$$.* A tremendous amount of research went into the preparation of this all new manual. Hundreds of man-hours and literally thousands of letters. Research has proved that this approach to earning extra income—even beginning a new career—is now a prime market. And, since our business is researching and presenting viable, profitable business opportunities to the public, we are delighted to make this new manual available.

COMMON SENSE AND PRACTICAL METHODS
If you're looking for a 'get rich quick' scheme, you can stop reading right now. Don't waste your time—or money—on this book. But, if you're genuinely interested in earning extra income for yourself and your family...and doing it in just a few spare hours each week ... and doing it from the privacy and comfort of your own home, then you should continue. Continue if you want to earn money easily and without any investment. This approach to an extra income is full of common sense and practical ways to earn money by clipping newspaper items.

TRADE SECRETS REVEALED
You learn exactly what kind of items to clip. And what not to clip. You discover how ordinary household supplies are used so you don't have to invest in lots of equipment and supplies.

Trade secrets known only to the few long time, established clipping bureaus are revealed to you. You even find out how to obtain other cities' newspapers absolutely free, in the event that you want to expand your business. You discover a little known trade secret that will allow you to be on retainer for $50-$300 per month, regardless of how many clippings you supply that month.

BIG BONUS
In addition to the complete instructions on selling clippings to magazines, you learn how to sell clippings to individuals. This vast market can double...even triple your earnings from selling to magazines. You use the same newspapers and many of the same materials. So earning even more money by incorporating this approach into your business is a cinch.

BUT THERE'S MORE
You get a complete package. Information on how to organize your business. Tax tips and how to take advantage of the tax savings your clipping business can generate. How to offset some of the 'ordinary income' from your or your spouse's regular job with perfectly legitimate tax deductions you would not otherwise have qualified for.

THERE'S STILL MORE!
You receive, absolutely free, a directory of magazines that purchase news clippings. Not just a listing, but many editors' names and addresses, what type of clippings each magazine is interested in and how much they pay for news items that you send them.

MORE BONUSES
You'll find ten more bonuses in the supplement ... all completely free. Instructions on how to sell to groups, how to sell older news items, how to find the addresses of prospects. Newsbreaks, photographs, and much more.

START NOW
BEGIN EARNING QUICKLY
Why wait? You can start within a couple of hours after you've received and read this informative and comprehensive manual. Age, education and experience are no barrier. Smaller towns and big cities are both excellent territories. This could be the start of a very successful small business for you and an excellent way to generate additional income for your family. Easy, fun, run from the privacy of your home and most of all ... profitable!

NOTHING ELSE TO BUY
You can begin with ordinary household items you already own. Supplies you purchase are inexpensive and go a long way. We have nothing else to sell you. You can begin in full confidence that we have conducted exhaustive research into this field and give this business opportunity our 'gold star' rating.

UNCONDITIONAL GUARANTEE
Your money back if you are not completely satisfied. It's as simple as that. No questions asked. We don't *have* to make this strong a guarantee ... because we know this manual is everything we say it is, and more. But we do. You have a full 30 days to examine the book. Analyze it. Try it. If you're not convinced within that time, just return it and you'll receive a full refund within five days. You don't receive many *can't lose* offers like this. Jump on it. Mail your order today. Just detach the coupon and mail to our address below with your $12.95.

Mail to:

National Paperback Books, Inc

[ ] YES! Rush my copy of *How to Turn Your Newspapers Into $$$$ Cash $$$$* complete with all bonuses. Enclosed is my $11.95 plus $1.00 p&h (total $12.95). #1604
[ ]Check; [ ]Money order;

Name_____

Address_____

City_____

State_____ Zip_____

TN residents add 7% sales tax

Advertisement   Advertisement   Advertisement

JOIN GAIL HOWARD'S GROWING LIST OF
LOTTO JACKPOT WINNERS

With her long-awaited book:

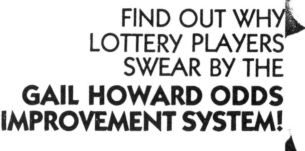

Gail Howard

FIND OUT WHY LOTTERY PLAYERS SWEAR BY THE GAIL HOWARD ODDS IMPROVEMENT SYSTEM!

Only $14.95

10 DOCUMENTED JACKPOT WINNERS HAVE WON MORE THAN $30 MILLION USING GAIL HOWARD'S SYSTEMS.

Now with this comprehensive 228 page book, LOTTO: HOW TO WHEEL A FORTUNE, you can learn over 100 Wheeling and Odds Improvement Systems from the nation's original Lottery expert, Gail Howard

ONLY GAIL HOWARD'S WHEELING SYSTEMS GIVE YOU:

* Built-In Balanced Games™
* VALID Guaranteed Minimum Win Assurances
* Maximum Number of Multiple Wins Possible With Each System
* *Exact* Guaranteed Odds Improvement Percentages ™ up to 667%
* Systems' Timetable for Getting 4, 5 or 6 Winning Numbers in Any Lotto Game
* Plus...Power Number Systems ™ to wheel more numbers for less money
* Plus...Balanced Wheeling Systems for Pick-5 and Pick-7 Lotto games

The Balanced Wheeling Systems found only in this book **MAKE ALL OTHER WHEELING SYSTEMS OBSOLETE.**

* No longer will you have to pay for tickets with unbalanced, wasted combinations.
* No more laborious wondering where to place your number combinations. Simply group your numbers low to high...The system tells you to rest.

* No more long complicated instructions. This new simple method makes it simple for anyone to wheel Lotto numbers.

Only Gail Howard's book of Wheeling Systems will give you the exact odds improvement percentages for specific systems...

STOP RELYING ON DUMB LUCK TO WIN AT LOTTERY

* You will be told exactly how often you can expect to win when you wheel from 7 to 24 Lotto numbers.
* You get not only your **Guaranteed Minimum Win Assurances** ™ but will be told the maximum you can possibly win with every system used!
* You get **Power Number Systems** ™ that let you play more numbers for less money with the same win guarantees.
* New systems for 5-number and 7-number games assure that Gail's Systems will work with any Lotto game in the world.

This valuable book is the most important tool for Lottery players to increase their chances of winning.

More than one and a half years of round-the-clock computer analysis have gone into research for **LOTTO: HOW TO WHEEL A FORTUNE.** The book was checked and rechecked after it was typeset to assure you that it contains no mistakes or printing errors in the Systems.

Remember: Only the **GAIL HOWARD WHEELING SYSTEMS** can claim exact **Odds Improvement Percentages** ™ for **Specific Wheeling Systems** and BACK IT UP WITH PROOF.

NOW AVAILABLE FOR YOUR COMPUTER

All the original, authentic Gail Howard systems are now available on IBM PC and compatibles; menu driven (user friendly).

Gail Howard's Smart Luck Computer Wheel™ ($29.95 + $2 s h) has a unique built-in Balanced Game™ feature which makes all other wheeling systems obsolete. Over 100 Wheeling Systems with minimum win guarantees; never before has a computer wheeling system offer so much. System also checks for wins.

Gail Howard's Smart Luck Computer Advantage™ ($39.95 + $2 s h) has the most successful number selection systems ever devised for beating the odds in Lotto. Includes the entire winning numbers list for one Lotto game of your choice. ($7 for each *additional* Lotto game). Available for any state or international Lotto game. **Please specify which Lotto game(s).**

SMART LUCK PUBLISHERS

☐ Yes! I want to dramatically improve my chances of winning at LOTTERY. Please send me Gail Howard's LOTTO: HOW TO WHEEL A FORTUNE.
I have enclosed my check or money order for **$14.95 + $2.00** s/h for each book.

☐ Smart Luck Computer Wheel $29.95 + $2.00 S/H   ☐ Smart Luck Computer Advantage $39.95 + $2.00 S/H

LOTTO game played _____

Name _____

Address _____

City _____ State _____ Zip _____

SMART LUCK PUBLISHERS
WIN LOTTO BY MATHEMATICAL PROBABILITY NOT BY CHANCE

Famous songwriter reveals secrets:

HOW TO WRITE A HIT SONG AND SELL IT

Do you like music? Do you like to sing? Do you write poems? Do you play a musical instrument? Would you like to write a hit song? If your answer is yes to any of these questions and if you are willing to devote some time to a pleasant and fun-filled hobby, you can be successful in the exciting world of music. Your dreams of song-writing success can come true! Listen to this.

SONGWRITER WITH 22 GOLD RECORDS TELLS YOU HOW

Tommy Boyce, an internationally well-known songwriter, has written a how-to book for the beginner or the up-and-coming songwriter called HOW TO WRITE A HIT SONG & SELL IT. In it he reveals professional song-writing tips and charts a course of instruction for you to follow. He tells you how he wrote six of his biggest hits and has even included the music and lyrics for you to study, sing and play. This fabulous book, which includes many personal photos of celebrities plus royalty statements from around the world, tells it all.

Here are some of the hit songs that Tommy Boyce has written:
LAST TRAIN TO CLARKSVILLE . . . COME A LITTLE BIT CLOSER . . . I WANNA BE FREE . . . VALLERI . . . I WONDER WHAT SHE'S DOING TONIGHT . . . LAZY ELSIE MOLLY . . . BE MY GUEST . . . PRETTY LITTLE ANGEL EYES . . . ALICE LONG . . . I'M NOT YOUR STEPPING STONE . . . PEACHES 'N' CREAM . . . WORDS . . . SHE . . . THEME FROM THE MONKEES
PLUS: The theme song for the ever-popular T.V. show THE DAYS OF OUR LIVES
Plus: His latest songs:
WILLIE BURGUNDY . . . WHO WANTS A SLIGHTLY USED WOMAN? . . . I WANNA BELIEVE IN LOVE

For the first time a famous songwriter shares what he has learned in his 17 years of writing hit songs year after year.
Here's the table of contents:
1. WHO AM I? 2. CAN THE AMATEUR SONG-WRITER REACH STARDOM? 3. HOW TO BEGIN WITH OR WITHOUT A MUSICAL BACKGROUND 4. MOODS, TITLES, AND MELODIES 5. WHERE DO SONGS COME FROM? 6. WHICH COMES FIRST, THE LYRICS OR THE MELODY? 7. ANALYZING HIT SONGS 8. WHAT MAKES A HIT SONG? 9. PROFESSIONAL SONG-WRITING TIPS FOR THE AMATEUR OR THE UP-AND-COMING SONGWRITER 10. HOW I CREATED SIX OF MY HIT SONGS 11. EVALUATING YOUR MUSIC 12. RE-WRITING BEFORE PRESENTING YOUR SONG 13. PROMOTING YOUR OWN SONG 14. COPYRIGHT, ASCAP, BMI 15. THE BUSINESS SIDE OF MUSIC 16. HOW TO SELL YOUR SONG IN PERSON OR BY MAIL 17. TOMMY BOYCE SONGWRITERS' CLUB 18. DIRECTORY OF RECORD COMPANIES 19. DIRECTORY OF MUSIC PUBLISHERS

YOU CAN BE A SUCCESSFUL SONGWRITER

Another invaluable book for every songwriter is the SONGWRITERS' RHYMING DICTIONARY containing thousands of rhymes which will be of tremendous help in your lyric writing. With it you can easily rhyme any word.

AN EXCITING, PROFITABLE SONG-WRITING FUTURE CAN BE YOURS

Wilshire Book Company, now in its 25th year, the publisher of these books and other best-selling books such as PSYCHO-CYBERNETICS, THINK & GROW RICH, A GUIDE TO RATIONAL LIVING, MAGIC OF THINKING BIG, and THREE MAGIC WORDS, stands behind this offer. You'll be encouraged in your own writing by an almost unbelievable musical success story of Melvin Powers, publisher, Wilshire Book Company, who as a direct result of reading Tommy Boyce's book in its manuscript form, recently wrote a song entitled MR. SONGWRITER which became a best seller on the country western charts. What this remarkable, instructive book did for new amateur songwriter, Melvin Powers, it can do for you.

Best of all, you'll have the opportunity of joining, without charge, the Tommy Boyce Songwriters' Club which is designed for all who have a genuine interest in music and seek the opportunity to write songs for fun and profit.

Don't delay. Get started in the fascinating world of song writing and music. Send today for HOW TO WRITE A HIT SONG & SELL IT, price $8.00 postpaid, plus SONGWRITERS' RHYMING DICTIONARY, price $8.00

30 DAY NO-RISK COUPON

National Paperback

Please rush:
☐ HOW TO WRITE A HIT SONG & SELL IT $8.00
☐ SONGWRITERS' RHYMING DICTIONARY . . . $8.00
It must start me on the road to becoming a hit songwriter or I may return the books within 30 days for a full refund
Enclosed is my check ☐   money order ☐ for $ _____

Name _____
(Please print)
Address _____
City _____ State _____ Zip _____

Tennessee residents add 7% sales tax./Add $1 per book for shipping & handling.

NOW, YOU CAN boost response, build profits, and achieve your hard-earned share of . . .

MAIL ORDER SUCCESS

by owning, studying, and applying the proven success principles in these uncommonly effective mail order success guides.

Master the
59 RESPONSE/PROFIT TIPS, TRICKS, & TECHNIQUES TO HELP YOU ACHIEVE MAJOR MAIL ORDER SUCCESS
$11

You get one specific mail order success tip, trick, & technique after another, each designed to put key response/profit knowledge in your head and increasingly large amounts of money in your pocket.

You'll get tips explaining how to boost response & profits from your ads & direct mail. You'll learn tricks used by direct response experts to make customers order repeatedly. And, you'll have fingertip access to the simple, but oh-so powerful, techniques used to subtly command an order from your prospect.

You'll discover how to create potent copy, construct money-making offers, select key mailing lists, obtain testimonials, maximize the value of each customer, make critical "go/no go" decisions, and so much more.

RECOMMENDED FOR: Emerging mail order entrepreneurs who want concise, precise, and proven response/profit tips without spending months in research and testing.

Learn
HOW TO WRITE AND DESIGN MONEY-MAKING RESPONSE ADVERTISEMENTS
$11

With little effort, you'll begin writing & designing ads that will "knock the response socks off" the ads you're currently using.

You'll eliminate response-killing mistakes... and replace them with proven response-building techniques.

Once you finish reading this Mail Order Success guide, you'll know how to create ads that . . . Capture ATTENTION . . . Spark INTEREST . . . Build DESIRE . . . and Generate ACTION . . . in the form of an order.

You'll discover the secrets of creating a winning headline, potent copy, powerful offer, eye-appealing graphics, & action-commanding order coupon. You'll learn how to use eye-directional devices, involvement devices, color, and unbalanced design. Plus, much more.

Ad creation trade secrets from basic concepts to sophisticated techniques.

RECOMMENDED FOR: Mail marketers who use space ads and who want substantial response/profit improvement.

Discover
HOW TO MAKE THE SUCCESSFUL TRANSITION FROM SMALL-TIME TO BIG-TIME MAIL ORDER
$11

You'll master the step-by-step specialized knowledge needed to transform your emerging, limited budget mail order business into a thriving mail order success story.

From mental preparation and pinpoint planning to creating advertising that hits the profit "bulls-eye" to snatching success from failure, you'll get specific strategies that are . . . BOLD yet safe . . . ADVANCED yet simple . . . POTENT yet easy-to-apply . . . POWERFUL yet inexpensive.

All of the "successful transition" concepts, strategies, and techniques are clearly explained so you can begin tapping them immediately. They'll help you mastermind your own successful transition . . . guaranteed or your money back.

RECOMMENDED FOR: Limited budget entrepreneurs intent on making their mail order operation a big-time success.

Isn't it time you achieved greater mail order success

20% OFF SPECIAL OFFER
Select all three guides and invest just $25.

FREE with each guide you select:
One back issue of MAIL ORDER CONNECTION... the professional mail marketer's how-to newsletter of effective response/profit techniques. You'll discover key success concepts, strategies, and techniques in a concise, easy-to-understand, easy-to-apply language to help you grab your share of the mail order profits.

Don't wait.
Request your Mail Order Success guides now. Order from:

National Paperback Books, Inc

MAIL ORDER SUCCESS SELECTION COUPON

☐ **RUSH** me the Mail Order Success guides checked off below, plus my FREE issue(s) of "Mail Order Connection." Don't forget my 30-day money-back guarantee.

Qty.	Title		Ea.	Total
	How To Write & Design Response Ads	#1743	**$11**	
	59 Tips, Tricks, & Techniques	#1741	**$11**	
	How To Make Successful Transition	#1742	**$11**	
	All Three Guides — Save 20%	#1749	**$25**	
		Total Enclosed		

Tennessee residents add 7% sales tax./Add $1 per book for shipping & handling

NAME: _____

ADDRESS: _____

CITY/STATE/ZIP: _____

Have You Ever Bowled A Strike And Said, "I've Got It!"?

What would your score be if you could bowl, all the time, with that same feeling? Pretty good? What would you say if we promised you that high score? Unbelievable? Incredible as it may seem, that is exactly what we promise.

If you are willing to keep an open mind for a new concept while you read this advertisement, we can point a way to help you improve your bowling score immeasurably as well as your enjoyment of the game.

The Mental Side of Bowling Crystallized into a Workable Formula

Have you ever rolled a gutter ball while concentrating on the theories of the proper stance, delivery, slide, release and follow-through? You know all there is to know about the mechanics of the bowling delivery and can recite the theories forwards and backwards. The only thing you don't seem to understand is your score. It seems the more you know and the harder you try, the worse you get.

If it is true that you know the fundamental movements of the bowling delivery and yet fail to bowl well, your failure must be in your mental play.

Here Is a Promise for Better Bowling

The pages of a new bowling book are dedicated to the mental side of bowling or, more specifically, to the use of self-hypnosis for control of the mechanical action of the bowling delivery. The use of self-hypnosis is a new concept and one that will help the bowler with all phases of his game. The reader will learn about the simplest, most effective technique ever devised to help him bowl consistently high scores.

What Will They Think of Next?

Your first reaction to the use of hypnosis for improving your bowling game will probably be a big smile followed by the comment, "What will they think of next?" Let us examine some interesting facts.

Book stores and libraries have racks filled with volumes on the physical side of bowling. Autobiographies by professional bowlers reveal, with the frankness of confession story writers, how they "feel" during every movement. Endless "tips" appear in newspapers and magazines aimed at improving the game of the average player.

Yet, why are there so many players seriously seeking improvement when the bowling delivery has been completely revealed, charted and plotted with the thoroughness of a geographical map?

The average player knows the fundamental movements of the bowling delivery, yet fails to play well. It must follow that his failure is in his mental play. Through hypnosis, the way to obtain a mental effect may be explained, understood and put to use. It reveals the mental side of bowling with the clarity that high speed cameras disclose the physical movements of the delivery.

Here's the Secret

Self-hypnosis helps the bowler to attain "the subconscious feel" which is imperative to good bowling. The subconscious feel has been described as the rhythm you have during a practice delivery, or that "sweet feeling" when a ball is thrown correctly. Any conscious effort usually produces muscle tension. This is what is meant when you are told "you are trying too hard." Your conscious mind is so concerned with the mechanical movements and your desire to spill the pins that it repeatedly produces muscle tension.

Use Your Practice Game in League Play

Keeping that important feeling is what you are going to learn from using self-hypnosis. It is the secret of the champions and high average bowlers who have discovered the means of taking their practice games into tournament and league play.

It is known as "the subconscious feel." Once you have learned how to activate this subconscious feeling and to bowl with the timing, relaxation and coordination possible in practice while under the tension of competition, most of your problems will be solved and you'll be well on the way to the high average you are capable of carrying.

The Experts Agree

Take it from Enrico (Hank) Marino, undefeated world champion, named Bowler of the Half-Century and a member of the Bowling Hall of Fame. Hank says, "It isn't until a bowler enters a tournament of competition, no matter how small it may be, that the mental side of the game asserts itself.

"The one thing that is impressive is the incredible change of temperament. This change of mental attitude almost makes a bowler a stranger to himself."

The great bowling master, Joe Falcaro, explains it as, "The kegler who feels he has a 300 game in the offing after two or three successive strikes will discover that every delivery gets tougher. His relaxation turns to tension and his muscles tighten. The ball seems to get heavier and more difficult to release. That's the mental side of bowling."

Every star writing on bowling or lecturing at clinics stresses that form is a highly individual matter. The only thing that really counts is being able to relax tension for a smooth delivery.

Carmen Salvino, who started bowling at 12, was in a Classic league at 17 and at 19 was the youngest American Bowling Congress (ABC) titlist, states: "I practice until the game becomes automatic. I don't have to think about what I intend to do with the ball, so I can be completely relaxed and natural when I am in competition."

Here's More Proof From the Experts

You could go right through the Bowling Hall of Fame and get identical advice from each of the greats. Ed Lubanski, Bowler of the Year in 1959, says, "Think what you are going to do as you take your stance. Then, don't think about anything in particular and just learn to spill the pins."

Only the phrasing changes as each of the champions gives advice. Buzz Fazio states it as, "Timing can make or break a bowler. The path to the foul line is short but is strewn with pitfalls if your timing is off.

Avoid stiffening. Be calm, relaxed and don't hurry your delivery."

The application of hypnosis to your bowling game was explained by Joseph Whitney in his popular King Features syndicated newspaper column, "Mirror of Your Mind." He wrote: "Properly performed, hypnosis is capable of changing mental attitudes at the conscious level. If faulty mental attitudes are responsible for an athlete's inadequate performance, a change wrought by hypnosis could improve his skill."

You Can Use Your Subconscious Mind for Better Bowling

Should the term hypnosis connotate mystery, black magic, stage trickery or fear, disregard it. Upon closer examination, you will find you are not only familiar with it, but you have been using it while thinking of it in other terms such as self-discipline, positive thinking, automatic response, muscle memory, suggestion or unconscious desire.

Hypnosis is not a new phenomenon. Its recorded history goes much further back in time than that of the ancient and honorable game of bowling.

The only thing new about hypnosis is when you, yourself, become aware of it. Then, its great power to influence the mind becomes known to you. You will learn to use it effectively, because you will understand how to channel its forces to tap the hidden resources of your subconscious mind. With the proper application of self-hypnosis, you will be able to bowl the best game you are physically capable of playing. The method of accomplishing this will be as normal as the automatic response while walking.

Try It Entirely At Our Risk!

We know you may be hesitant about trying this new approach and because of this we make the following offer:

TRY THE INSTRUCTIONS FOR 30 DAYS. See for yourself the unbelievable results. If you don't score higher, bowl consistently better and derive greater satisfaction from your bowling game — simply return the book for every cent of your money back. Fair enough?

The sound, authoritative instructions for using self-hypnosis to improve your bowling are presented in a clear, logical sequence and packed with new bowling aids in the book, HOW YOU CAN BOWL BETTER USING SELF-HYPNOSIS, by Jack Heise.

You have absolutely nothing to lose! Act today!

------ MAIL NO-RISK COUPON TODAY! ------

National Paperback Books, Inc

Gentlemen: Send me a copy of Jack Heise's amazing book, HOW YOU CAN BOWL BETTER USING SELF-HYPNOSIS.

I will use this book for 30 days entirely at your risk. If I do not score higher, I will simply return the book for a full refund.

Enclosed is my check ☐   money-order ☐ for $5.95

Name _____

Address _____

City _____ State _____ Zip _____

Tennessee residents add 7% sales tax./Add $1 per book for shipping & handling.

TABLE OF CONTENTS

INTRODUCTION

CONCLUSION

BOOKS: Samples

ADVERTISING: Samples

Notes

Notes

Notes

19361
(4) Mars 1991